IN THE BEGINNING
Genesis Chapters 1 to 3 and the Authority of Scripture

E. J. YOUNG

THE BANNER OF TRUTH TRUST

THE BANNER OF TRUTH TRUST
3, Murrayfield Road, Edinburgh EH12 6EL
P.O. Box 621, Carlisle, Pennsylvania 17013, USA

*

© The Banner of Truth Trust, 1976
First published 1976
ISBN 0 85151 235 6

*

Set in 11 on 13 point Garamond
and printed and bound in Great Britain by
Hazell Watson & Viney Ltd, Aylesbury, Bucks

Contents

Publishers' Preface

*T*wo books on chapters in the Book of Genesis were published by E. J. Young in his lifetime, *Studies in Genesis One* in 1964,[1] and *Genesis 3*,[2] a devotional and expository study, in 1966. He died two years after the publication of the second title at the age of sixty. The appearance of this further material by him at this date will not therefore be expected and it requires explanation. Dr. Young did not prepare these pages for publication; they are the *spoken* word addressed to the students of Toronto Baptist Seminary over the period March 20–24, 1967, and subsequently printed *verbatim* in *The Gospel Witness*, Toronto, in a series which ran from July 1967 to January 1968. With a minimum of editing these addresses are here reprinted from that source.

Two features call for comment. First, as these were popular addresses, not academic lectures, the mode of presentation will be found to have a very general appeal. Nothing was of greater concern to Dr. Young in the last year of his life than that the Church should speak plainly

1. The Presbyterian and Reformed Publishing Company.
2. The Banner of Truth Trust.

and forcibly on the inspired record of man's creation and fall. He deplored the suggestion that there are complexities and obscurities in the meaning of Genesis chapters 1 to 3 which excuse us from holding and expressing clear-cut convictions. These pages are a memorable example of the manner in which true apologetics should be conducted.

Secondly, the author's main theme is the authority of Scripture. Not to give a verse-by-verse commentary on three chapters but to evaluate those features of the biblical text which have been most commonly subjected to doubt or denial, was his aim. He shows how a full acceptance of the divine authority of the Bible is both consistent with the Genesis narrative and necessary to its proper interpretation. Much has been written on this subject in recent years but the present publishers know of nothing more helpful for the general Christian public than these pages.

Gratitude is due to *The Gospel Witness* for the survival of this material and for allowing the republication of these addresses. Thanks are also expressed to the Presbyterian and Reformed Publishing Company for permitting the extract on the Westminster Confession and the Covenant of Works, taken from *Scripture and Confession*, 1973.

It is to be regretted that no biography of E. J. Young has appeared since his death and as many readers may have limited knowledge of his life we conclude this preface with an Appreciation written by John Murray in 1968. Young had studied under Murray at Westminster Theological Seminary, Philadelphia in the early 1930's, and from the time of his appointment as Professor in Old Testament in 1936 until Murray left Westminster in

December 1966 the two were close colleagues, both in the Seminary and in the witness of the Orthodox Presbyterian Church. Since the following was written John Murray has also – on May 8, 1975 – fallen asleep in Christ:

'On Wednesday, the 14th of February, Edward J. Young was called hence to be with the Lord. The end of his earthly pilgrimage by a heart attack came unexpectedly. The church of God on earth has lost one of its most devoted ornaments and the cause of Reformed scholarship one of its most erudite and consecrated exponents. It was an inestimable privilege to have been closely associated with Dr. Young for some thirty years as a colleague at Westminster Seminary. In the last four years before retirement from my work at the Seminary I was deeply impressed by the evidence my friend gave of the maturing fruit of the Spirit. But little did I think that he was being rapidly prepared for the immediate presence of the Saviour whom he loved and whose glory he delighted to proclaim. We had all expected many more years of his devoted labour.

'Edward J. Young adorned his Christian profession. So many were the virtues making up this adornment that it is difficult to single out any for special appreciation. But his humility was so conspicuous that no one could fail to mark it. For those who knew him more intimately his circumspect consistency was no less evident. Unassuming, and reluctant to make his own voice heard, he was always ready to speak out when the honour of Christ and the claims of truth demanded it. He burned with holy jealousy for the integrity of God's Word and for the maintenance of the whole counsel of God.

'Dr. Young was an untiring worker. His literary output was prodigious. Those acquainted with his many contributions to Old Testament studies soon discovered the thoroughness of his preparation and the breadth of his scholarship. His linguistic talent was phenomenal. He was master of Hebrew and Aramaic, and with the Semitic languages bearing upon Old Testament studies he was thoroughly conversant. But not only were the ancient tongues his province. He read with ease a great variety of modern languages and thus no significant phase of Old Testament study escaped his notice or failed to receive his assessment. His greatest undertaking was a three-volume commentary on the Book of Isaiah. The first volume appeared in 1965, the second is apparently about to be issued.[1] How far advanced was the work on the third volume I am unable to say. No one living today surpassed Dr. Young in reliable, well-informed, and well-considered judgment on questions related to the Old Testament.

'The distinction for which, above all others, Dr. Young should be commended and remembered as a scholar is the reverence he entertained for Scripture as the Word of God. To the defence of the Bible as such, and to its exposition as the living Word of the living God, he devoted all his talents and energies. Destructive criticism of the Scripture he resisted to the utmost. The Bible he believed was revelation from God, always relevant and by the Holy Spirit sealed in our hearts to be what it intrinsically is, the inerrant Word of God. That this was the

---

1. It was published in 1969 (William B. Eerdmans) and the third volume, the manuscript of which Dr. Young had completed shortly before his death, appeared in 1972.

controlling factor in Dr. Young's thinking is evident in all of his writings and the devotion it implied and produced is demonstrated in what may be regarded as his more devotional volumes. He knew nothing of an antithesis between devotion to the Lord and devotion to the Bible. He revered the Bible because he revered the Author. And he revered and served the God of Scripture because he was captive to Scripture as revelatory Word.

'The influence exerted by Edward J. Young will continue through the many books and articles that came from his pen. Supreme wisdom and love ordained his removal from our midst. Before the Lord's sovereign will we must bow in humble resignation and also with gratitude upon every remembrance of the Saviour's grace in and to our departed friend. "Blessed are the dead which die in the Lord from henceforth: Yea, saith the Spirit, that they may rest from their labours; and their works do follow them" (Rev. 14:13).'

1. Introductory

ONE thing that everyone can do is raise questions about the first chapter of Genesis, and right at the outset I want to say that there are a great many questions that we simply cannot answer. There is the old matter of the relationship between this first chapter and that which scientists are saying; but I think even more significant to-day is the question as to the nature of this first chapter. We have all heard the term 'myth' that is applied to it and used very widely to-day. It is therefore very important that we consider the nature of this first chapter of Genesis.

Genesis is Scripture

First, just a few preliminary remarks about the Book of Genesis. Its first chapter, just as much as everything else in Genesis, is a portion of the Holy Scriptures, and Paul has told us that 'all scripture is God-breathed'. I think that when Paul makes that statement he has in mind the Book of Genesis just as much as any other part of Scripture. We are not therefore simply dealing with some document that happens to have come down to us from times of antiquity.

The Babylonians had such a document. Other ancient peoples had such documents. We are not simply dealing with a cosmogony of the ancient Hebrews. We are dealing with a book that belongs to the Holy Scriptures; and the statement of the Apostle Paul, 'All scripture is given by inspiration of God', or 'All scripture is God-breathed', applies to the Book of Genesis just as much as it does to any other part of God's Book.

Now that is going to colour my views. I am going to regard Genesis as Scripture. I am adopting a presupposition here. All of us have presuppositions whether we realize it or not. There is no such thing as approaching the Bible or Christianity with a perfectly neutral mind to find out what the truth is. I know we deceive ourselves sometimes by thinking that we can do that, but we cannot. We are either for Christ or against him, and we either regard the Bible as the Word of God, or we do not regard it as the Word of God. To avoid any misunderstandings at the start of our enquiries, I want to make it very clear where I stand on this matter. I do regard Genesis as sacred Scripture.

Genesis is Unique

When we look at the first chapter of Genesis we realize right away that it is unique. People are asking what is its literary value, that is, what kind of writing is it? The modern school of Biblical criticism—though it is not so modern after all—maintains that every bit of writing in the Old Testament (and the New Testament as well) must be categorized. There is a certain type to which it belongs, so we are told, and we must endeavour to discover what that type is. There are creation stories, cosmogonies, that come from the ancient world, and we must see how Genesis chapter one fits in with these. I want to say right away that I think Genesis one is unique. There is no parallel to it. If you would compare it —and we shall have to make some comparisons—with what the Babylonians have left us concerning the origin of the world, or the Sumerians, or the Egyptians, or anybody else, you would find that the first chapter of Genesis stands out like a fair flower in a barren wilderness. And that is a question that every one of us has to face. How do you account for the uniqueness of the Book of Genesis, the first book of the Bible? What is your explanation?

Explanations are given from a variety of quarters, but I only intend to mention one of them as an example, and it is that given by Professor von Rad and other German scholars. I give it in very simple form. What they say is that not all the Israelites were in the Egyptian captivity. Six of the tribes had never been in Egypt. They were in Palestine. The Leah and the Rachel tribes, who had been in Egypt, united with them later. That which united these twelve tribes was religion. It was their God, Jahveh, as they called Him, and their belief in this one particular God, that caused a loose confederation of states to be formed. Here they were, then, in Palestine, and they were subject to influences from without, especially from their Canaanitish neighbours. The Canaanites were polytheists. They had a nature worship, and there was great danger that this would be taken over by the Israelites, and that the distinctiveness of the Israelites would be destroyed. But there were priests of the Jahveh congregations who saw to it that polytheistic elements would be rejected in anything that was taken over from the Canaanites. And so, among other things, you have an account of the creation. It goes back to Mesopotamia originally, but is mediated through the Canaanites, and as it was taken over by these Israelitish groups the priests purified it more and more as the years passed. They cut out from it polytheistic accretions, until finally you have the first chapter of Genesis.

The German scholars go further. They tell the world that the first chapter of Genesis is an amalgam of two basic accounts—an account of action, that is to say, a deed account, and also a word account. The deed account is 'And it was so', 'And God divided', 'And the earth brought forth', and so on. The word account is 'And God said' . . . 'And God said'. These two basic accounts were amalgamated with the result that what we have to-day in the first chapter of Genesis is not at all a revelation of God which was written down by Moses, but rather the so-called priestly document of creation.

Now I know full well that I have given a very sketchy account of the German view, the German explanation of the first chapter of Genesis. But it is an explanation that does not explain. It is not at all a satisfactory account of how and why the Hebrews could produce such a cosmogony. Why is it that the Hebrews could produce so pure a document whereas other people of antiquity, far better educated and with a greater civilization, were unable to do it? These early Hebrews were not advanced much beyond the Bedouin of to-day who live in Palestine. They were not people from whom you would expect any great cultural advance at all. Why is it, then, that they could produce the first chapter of Genesis, whereas the Babylonians and the Egyptians and the others could not do it? Even Ovid's *Metamorphoses*, which is a highly developed work, could come up with nothing better than the polytheism that characterizes it. What is the explanation?

I do not think that these modern German explanations explain anything. They are theories and nothing more. They leave us still with the question, how do you explain the first chapter of Genesis? I think that our best apologetic is to take the offensive. I do not mean that we must be offensive. It is easy enough for us to be offensive, and I fear that sometimes we descend to it in our defence of Christianity. But we have every right to challenge the unbelieving thought of the modern day; and when that thought comes up with explanations of the phenomena of the Bible, it is our duty to challenge that thought with some of the questions that we can raise. And this surely is an important question—How do you explain the uniqueness of this first chapter of Genesis?

Fiat and Fulfilment

The chapter begins with a general statement—'God created the heaven and the earth'. Notice that the account is given in terms of what we may call 'fiat' and 'fulfilment'. By the term 'fiat' I simply mean, 'Let it be'. And so you read throughout the chapter, 'And God said'. 'And God said, Let there be light'. 'And God said, Let there be an expanse'. 'And God said, Let the waters be gathered together unto one place', and so on. This fiat is completed by a fulfilment, and the fulfilment is expressed in such terms as 'And there was light', 'And God divided the waters', 'And the earth caused to go forth the grass', and so on. And then quite often you find the statement added, 'And it was so', as if to point out the ease with which God could accomplish these things.

The first chapter of Genesis, then, gives the account of creation in terms of what we may well call 'fiat' and 'fulfilment', and this is really unique. I am well aware that in some Sumerian documents there are statements that seem to suggest a fiat, but there is really nothing that is comparable to what you have in the first chapter of Genesis. So I repeat that Genesis chapter one gives us fiat, fulfilment, and then the summing up of it all in the words 'And it was so'.

Divine Satisfaction

Furthermore, we may notice in this first chapter of Genesis the divine complacency, the divine satisfaction. So often we read, 'And God saw that it was good'. The first such statement is given with respect to the light: 'And God saw the light that it was good', and the final statement appears in verse 31: 'And God saw everything that he had made, and, behold, it was very good.' The Creator rests satisfied with the creation, not because the creation is something good that exists apart from God, but because the creation was precisely what God wanted it to be. His will was accomplished, and he was satisfied in his own handiwork. The Psalmist sums it up in the words: 'He spake and it was done; he commanded and it stood fast' (Psalm 33:9).

Notice further the emphasis that is placed in this first

chapter of Genesis upon *God*. In every verse *God* is active. It is God and his monergism that stands before us. God created, God said, God saw, God divided, God called, and so on. And in the two occurrences where the word 'God' is not used as a subject, the phrase in which it occurs is used as a subject: 'The Spirit of God was hovering upon the waters'. It is God who is active in every one of these occurrences.

Here I want to prevent a misunderstanding. When I say that the first chapter of Genesis presents God as active, I do not mean this statement to be taken in the Barthian sense. I do not mean the activistic philosophy that has come upon the scene since the time of Kant. I do not mean activism as over against metaphysics. The Bible presents God as active, but it presents *God* as active: 'In the beginning *God* created'. The emphasis is not on creation alone. It is on God just as much as on the creation. It is God, as metaphysically distinct from us, who engaged in the work of creation. Such is the Biblical emphasis.

To-day we get an emphasis and a stress all the time upon the God who *acts*, not upon the God who is. We are told that the Hebrews never asked such questions. But how can anybody know to-day what kind of questions the ancient Hebrews asked? We are told that they were not interested in metaphysics, that they were not interested in the question, 'Who is God?', but only concerned in seeing God acting. Such is the modern view. But it is not the Biblical view at all. It is God who acts, and I am stressing the metaphysics here. It is God, God the Creator who is acting, but the chapter presents *this God* as the God who acts, and that is something quite different from the modern Barthian teaching.

The creation is described in what we may call paragraphs or strophes. It does not matter what language we use. Each one is described as a day, and there are six of these days in the first chapter of Genesis, and then on the seventh day, as mentioned in the second chapter of Genesis, God ceases from his work.

Is Genesis Poetry or Myth?

To escape from the plain factual statements of Genesis some Evangelicals are saying that the early chapters of Genesis are poetry or myth, by which they mean that they are not to be taken as straightforward accounts, and that the acceptance of such a view removes the difficulties. Some are prepared to say that difficulties about the resurrection of Christ are removed at once if you say that the writers of the Gospels do not mean us to understand that a miracle occurred, and that they are simply giving us a poetic account to show that Christ lives on. To adopt such a view, they say, removes all troubles with modern science. But the truth is that, if you accept such beliefs and methods, you are abandoning the Christian faith. If you act thus with Genesis you are not facing up to the facts, and that is a cowardly thing for Evangelicals to do. Genesis is not poetry. There are poetical accounts of creation in the Bible—Psalm 104, and certain chapters in Job—and they differ completely from the first chapter of Genesis. Hebrew poetry had certain characteristics, and they are not found in the first chapter of Genesis. So the claim that Genesis one is poetry is no solution to the question. The man who says, 'I believe that Genesis purports to be a historical account, but I do not believe that account', is a far better interpreter of the Bible than the man who says, 'I believe that Genesis is profoundly true, but it is poetry'. That latter has nothing to commend it at all. I disagree with the first man, but he is a better exegete, he is a better interpreter, because he is facing up to the facts. So I conclude that Evangelicals who want to hold to evolution as the unbeliever holds to it, and to get over the difficulties by saying that Genesis is to be interpreted as poetry or myth and not in a factual manner, cannot, in my view, be honest interpreters.

2. Verse one and the Chapter

IN order that we may understand
these matters a little more clearly we shall first of all
consider the relationship in which the first verse of
Genesis stands to the rest of the chapter. In the King
James version we read the simple declaration: 'In the
beginning God created the heaven and the earth'. It is a
very simple statement, and yet it is, perhaps, as profound
a statement as ever has been written. But certain modern
translations of the Bible begin quite differently. For
example, the Revised Standard Version, while translating
almost as does the King James Version, has a footnote
which says, 'When God began to create.' The Westminster Study Edition of the Holy Bible begins: 'When
God began to create the heaven and the earth', while the
Moffatt Bible starts with the words: 'This is the story of
how the universe was formed. When God began to form
the universe . . .' In other words, what these modern
versions do is to make a temporal clause out of the first
verse of Genesis. Now a temporal clause is not complete
in itself. It requires a further statement to complete its
meaning, and that further statement, they say, is found in

verse three: 'Then God said, Let there be light'. That is an independent statement and grammatically that can stand alone. But not only do we have a dependent statement and an independent statement; in between there is verse two, which is parenthetical and has to be paraphrased something like this: 'When God began to create the heaven and the earth, then the earth was without form and void, and darkness was upon the face of the abyss, and the Spirit of God was hovering over the waters; then God said, Let there be light'.

But what is involved if we translate the Hebrew in this way? It is very clear that if this view is correct—and it goes back to a Jewish exegete of the Middle Ages—then it denies absolute creation. If you say, When God began to create, the earth was always present 'without form and void', obviously there is no absolute creation, and by that I mean creation out of nothing. If the modern translations are correct, then when God began the work of creation, the material which he used was already present.

There was a German scholar, Hermann Gunkel, who said that it did not make any difference how you translated verse one. You could translate it as a temporal clause or as an independent statement. But it makes all the difference in the world. If what I am opposing is correct, then the first chapter of Genesis does not teach creation. So it is well that we look into the matter.

There is also another matter that we have to face. There is always the danger that we will mould the Bible to fit our theological statements. But the Bible is not to be manipulated so that it will support our theological position. Our theological position must be adjusted so that it will support what the Bible teaches. And that is why the theologian—and every Christian must be a theologian—must constantly examine his beliefs to see if what he believes is really what the Bible teaches. That is the way we have to proceed. Now if the Bible does not teach creation we have to let it go at that. It is not honest exegesis to force the Bible to say what we want it to say.

The Beginning and the Creation

I have simply been pointing out the consequences of what the view taken by the modern translators involves. But now we must go further and ask: 'What actually does the Bible teach—creation or otherwise?' How are we to regard the modern translations? To begin with, I must say that Julius Wellhausen, who can hardly be accused of orthodoxy, made the statement that the translation against which I raise grave objections was 'desperate'. Now I do not find that Wellhausen and I usually go hand in hand as far as Biblical matters are concerned, but at this point I thoroughly agree with him that this is a 'desperate' translation. I do not think it is correct at all. It is a grammatically possible translation, but to say that something is grammatically possible does not mean that it is necessarily correct. The modern translators proceed upon the assumption that the Hebrew demands their translation. That is not true. Elsewhere I have written on this matter in detail, but I will not do so here. Most people find that a discussion of Hebrew grammar is not a very scintillating matter. But I must point out one thing, namely, that the first two words of the Bible have a threefold alliteration.

The first word of the Bible begins with the letters that roughly correspond to our English B R A, and the second word of the Bible begins with these same three letters B R A. I think that this threefold alliteration is deliberate. It ties up these two words by showing that the explanation of the word 'create' is found in the word 'beginning', and the explanation of the word 'beginning' is found in the word 'create'.

Nevertheless, the Hebrew Massoretes have inserted an accent between those two words, which means that you must make a pause (we call it a disjunctive accent). They did not tie up these two words in the sense that the modern translations do. It is clear, then, that the words are to be separated, and all the ancient translations of the Bible do separate them, and translate them as a straightforward statement, 'In the beginning God created the heaven and the earth'. The real reason that lies behind the modern translations is that the Babylonian creation account, we are told, begins that way. Let us look at it. It starts out: 'When on high the heavens were not named, and below the earth had not a name', and then it goes on for seven lines. Then it proceeds with another temporal clause, and on the ninth line, it gives its main clause. That is to say, it begins with two long temporal dependent sentences and concludes on the ninth line with an independent statement. Hence, say the moderns, as the Babylonian creation account begins in that way, Genesis chapter one, being a similar cosmogony from the ancient world, must begin in the same way. Here is the real reason, I repeat, that leads so many men to-day to say that verse one must be construed as a temporal clause. The Hebrew does not begin that way, but it begins: 'In the beginning God created the heaven and the earth'.

I will not go into any greater detail, but would simply say that simplicity is the characteristic of Hebrew sentences. In German, for example, you have long involved temporal sentences, and you wait and wait until the finite verb finally comes. In Greek it is much the same, and also in Latin. You can follow the same practice in English, and in Babylonian, but it is very rare in Hebrew. Simplicity, co-ordination, is the characteristic of Hebrew sentences. If we take it as it stands, then, and I am going to let it go at that, we have a grand declaration of the fact of creation: 'In the beginning God created . . .'

The Absolute Beginning

The word 'beginning' is, of course, a relative term. It must imply the beginning of something. On that account, some say it refers only to the beginning of human history that we see unfolded round about us. But the content of the term is given to us by the word *bara'*, create, and vice versa. This is a beginning that is characterized by creation, and this is a creation that is characterized by the beginning. Here it means 'the absolute beginning'. This is widely accepted. It is not the view of conservative scholars alone. V. Schmidt has given his account of the creation in *The Priestly Code*, which is a very radical book. Nevertheless it interprets this phrase as referring to the absolute beginning. And when I was in Leipzig I heard Professor Karl Elliger expound this verse in the same way. It refers to the absolute beginning, just as John, beginning his Gospel, takes over the phrase 'In the beginning' and refers it to the absolute beginning. 'In the beginning God created', and the word for create that is employed here is a word that is used only with God as the subject. Never do we read in the Bible that a man creates. It is God who creates. He has created the heaven and the earth.

The Word 'Created'

Furthermore, the word is used of the production of something that is fundamentally new. God created the heaven and the earth. God created the great sea monsters. God created man. And in the latter part of the prophecy of Isaiah the word is used where God speaks of the creation of a new heaven and a new earth. Also, if a material is ever employed in the creation, that material is never mentioned. You never read in the Bible, for example, that God created man out of the dust of the ground. Instead we read: 'The Lord God *formed* man out of the dust of the ground' (Gen. 2:7). A different word is used. But the word *bara'* (create) is more restricted in its force than our English word 'create'. We use the word 'creation' rather broadly. We refer to almost anything as a creation, whether it be a motor-car or a house, or anything else, and only when we use it in a theological sense do we restrict its meaning to the doctrine of creation. But the Hebrew word *bara'* is used only with the restrictions that I have mentioned. So we are dealing here with the fact of absolute creation.

God and the World

'God created the heaven and the earth'. What do the words mean? We can perhaps get at the meaning by showing in the first place what the words do not mean. They do not mean that God formed a part of himself into the heavens and the earth. The heavens and the earth are not created from an emanation of God and are not an emanation of God. The words certainly do not mean that the material of creation was already present, but simply that God willed the existence of what formerly had no existence. You and I cannot grasp that, for we are finite, we are creatures. It is only God that can create, and this is, in a sense, the fundamental doctrine of all Christianity. When men speak about belief in God, what kind of a God are they talking about? Who is their God? The God of the Bible is the God who can create. It is well that we meditate on that for a moment, because the thought simply staggers us. *We* cannot create. If we want to make something we have to have the material, and then what we really do is form it or fashion it into something else. We are craftsmen, not creators. We cannot do what God has done; but Almighty God has simply willed that things come to pass, that they spring into existence, and we can only believe that because we trust God. We have faith in him. We do not know how it is possible. We cannot explain it. There are no analogies that would explain it. But we must believe it, otherwise whatever God we believe in is simply a part of the world process. He is part of that process in which we find ourselves engulfed, and if that is so, he is not a God that can help us. If he is only a little bigger than we are, if he is only a big brother and nothing more, if he is only a part of the whole, then we are all in it together, God, you and I, and then there are no standards. There is no absolute. It is every man for himself, and all modern philosophies and ideas that are being spread in our days—new morality, new theology, and so on—are all perfectly admissible if God is only a part of the world process. If it is so, it does not matter whether he is dead or alive, he cannot help us. Let us live for the moment, let us live for our enjoyment; there is no absolute; there is no standard of morality, for all changes. What may be right to-day may be wrong to-morrow; so let us get through life as best we can.

The Bible does not so speak. It tells us that God has created all things. That is why there is meaning in life, and why there are absolute standards that do not change. God tells us what is right and what is wrong, and that is why there is meaning in life. That is why you and I who believe in this God can very well say that our chief reason for existence is to glorify him and enjoy him for ever. If this God is the Creator, then we are to live for his glory. He created the heaven and the earth.

Notice the phrase 'the heaven and the earth'. It simply means all things, and in particular the earth. The word 'heaven' in this first verse of Genesis simply means 'all things apart from the earth'. The conjunction 'and' singles out this object. We have another example of this in the first verse of the Prophecy of Isaiah, where we are told that the vision is that which Isaiah saw concerning Judah and Jerusalem, that is, concerning Judah, and in particular, Jerusalem. And so God created the heaven, and in particular, the earth; and so the second verse in Genesis carries on the theme: 'And the earth . . .' I would say, then, that the first verse of Genesis chapter one is a general comprehensive statement of the fact of creation, such as is not found in the Babylonian account, or in any other account of antiquity. It comes to us only in this first chapter of Genesis.

3. Is Genesis One History?

I INTEND to go very rapidly through some of the remainder of the chapter. I believe that the detailed account begins with the second verse and that it concludes with the thirty-first verse, and that there is a contrast between verse two and verse thirty-one, a contrast that we can call 'chaos' and 'cosmos'. The chaos simply refers to the original unformed state of the earth, and cosmos to the well-finished universe. Here I find myself in agreement with Dr. von Rad, because he has brought this out rather forcefully in his commentary on Genesis, and I think this is a correct analysis of the form of these verses.

But when I say that verse two depicts chaos I want to guard against misconceptions. When you and I say something is in a state of chaos we mean that it is topsy-turvy, out of order. That is not what I mean here. I think Milton may perhaps have influenced us all a great deal by his *Paradise Lost*, but the Greek word *chaos* simply refers to the original unformed state of the earth. And so here in verse two it says: 'Now the earth was desolation and waste, and darkness was upon the face of the abyss. And the Spirit of God was hovering over the waters. Then God said, Let there be light . . .' That threefold description is, I say, a description of the unformed earth. At that time man could not have lived upon it. This does not mean that it was in any sense evil. We have here a threefold description, and grammatically we are to construe this with the verb in verse three—'God said, Let there be light', which clearly means that this threefold condition was in existence at the time when God said, 'Let there be light'. I think we have every reason to assume that this is the way the earth came from the hands of the Creator, that this threefold condition had existed from the point of absolute creation until the time when God said, 'Let there be light'. How long a time that was no man knows. I do not intend to say anything in particular about the restitution theory, which implies that there was a judgment of the original earth, that it was ruined, and that the remainder of the chapter describes a kind of re-creation. I do not think that this can be supported from the Scripture at all, and I intend to pass it by, because there are other questions that I consider more important, and it is these with which I wish to deal.

Think again of the statements in verse two: 'The earth was desolation and waste; darkness was upon the face of the abyss. And the Spirit of God was hovering over the waters'. Karl Barth says that this is not a description of a previous condition of the earth. He says that, if it is such a description, then you are faced with a dilemma. Either the earth came into this condition because God created it that way, or it came into this condition independently. He says that God did not create it in this way, because verse two

describes an evil condition. In this interpretation Barth
bases his exegetical remarks, as far as I am able to discern,
on a commentary of another German scholar. He asks
therefore what we are to do with this dilemma, and he
tells us there is an easy way out. If we interpret the verse
as referring not to a previous condition of the earth, but
simply to the previous condition of sin and evil, and what
the earth may fall back into again, then we no longer have
dilemma. But we have some other things that are far more
serious. At this point I shall have to introduce two
German words because Barth does so—Historie and
Geschichte. Most languages, except English, have two
words for history. 'Geschichte' simply means 'history' in
the English sense of that word, just as we would speak of
a 'history' of the German people. But Germans also have
this other word which is pronounced as either *Historie* or
Historia according to the different types of users of the
word.

Historie and Geschichte

If I understand the modern theology aright, *Historie* is
history in our sense. It is something that took place, and
it is history whether it is important or not. The fact that a
building caught fire three thousand years ago in some
place or other is history. It may not be so important as the
conquests of Julius Caesar, but it is just as historical. It
took place. But *Geschichte* according to Barth, if I understand him aright, and according to a great many others
too, is not that which took place upon this earth at all.
Geschichte is another kind of history. If you were to ask
Karl Barth positively what he means by the term, I do not

believe he has ever given an answer. But I think we have a way of discovering how the word is used, and I do not think that I misrepresent him. Modern philosophy and theology maintain that what we know round about us is the *phenomenon*. We learn of it through our sense, but this is not the real thing. This is what I know of it through my senses, but 'out there' in the noumenal realm is the thing in itself, the real thing. There is where God is, and about that 'out there' we can know nothing. And the realm of 'out there' is what they term *Geschichte*. That is why when neo-orthodox theology says, 'I believe in the resurrection of Christ', or 'I believe in the Virgin Birth of Christ', I am not impressed, for they do not believe that the resurrection and the Virgin Birth were *Historie* but *Geschichte*. They are 'out there'.

The United Presbyterian Church in the United States is deeply involved in the substitution of this modern religion for Christianity. Let me explain how it is doing it, because this will throw light on the modern approach to Genesis chapter one. Think of the difference in terms of God's reconciling act. You and I as Christians believe in God's reconciling act, and you and I know what it was. It occurred when the Lord Jesus Christ died on the cross of Calvary, when he satisfied the justice of God by the shedding of his precious blood. God, the offended Father, has been reconciled to his people, so that he may justly forgive them their sins, and we glory in the substitutionary atonement because of what Christ has done. The Bible says much about the matter, does it not? But the new Presbyterian confession tells us that God's reconciling act is a truth in the depths of God's love beyond the reach of theory, and that is saying exactly the same thing as if you were to say that it is in the noumenal. It is in *Geschichte*. Call it the depths of God's love if you will. If it is beyond the reach of theory, that means that we cannot say anything about it. It amounts to the substitution of modern theology for the Christian religion, the substitution of another god for the Triune God of the Bible. You and I know the Triune God and we can say all that about him that he has revealed concerning himself. You and I do know the reconciling act of God, and we can speak about all that God has revealed to us. But here is a great Presbyterian church having a new religion imposed upon it, and the average minister in that church does not seem to have the faintest idea of what is taking place.

To return—Barth says that the creation account is an account of *Geschichte* first of all, which means that there is no creation in the orthodox Christian sense of the term, and that it is being written in an unhistorical fashion. It comes to this, that Barth is rejecting the doctrine of creation in order that he may impose a modern philosophical view on the Book of Genesis. This is a very serious matter.

The Falsity of Barth's Interpretation

I have concentrated on Karl Barth's interpretation of this verse because his type of interpretation underlies a great deal that is being said about Genesis to-day. Barth maintains that the verse does not describe a condition in which the earth was once found, but that it is rather a condition of sin, of apostasy, or rebellion, and so on—a condition into which the earth can recede again. But this is not what the verse means. It is the imposition upon the text of a certain philosophical position which is very widespread to-day, and that undergirds the idea that the Hebrews, when they wanted to speak about creation, apparently could not speak in straightforward language, as you and I would do, but had to employ the concept of myth. I have never understood why that limitation had to be imposed upon the Hebrews. If they could not speak of creation in straightforward language, but were forced to employ myth, how is it that they can speak of God without using the concept of myth? How can they speak about sin and atonement, and so on, without using myth? All of the mysteries of the Christian faith *are* mysteries, and if we cannot speak about them in straightforward language, can we ever really be sure that we understand them at all? But I can see no reason why the Hebrews could not speak about creation in straightforward language. Genesis does just that. What we are faced with in our day is the imposition of a new theology or philosophy upon the Bible.

I hold a view of history entirely different from that which undergirds Barth's view. According to him, Genesis chapter one is an unhistorical writing of history, and it cannot be treated as relating to what actually transpired. On the contrary, it seems to me that our concept of history must be derived from the Scriptures themselves. That is historical which actually took place, whether you and I can control it or not. It is historical, not because some document remains to tell us that it took place, but it is historical if it ever did take place.

Now how do we know that the events recorded in the

CHAPTER 3

first chapter of Genesis actually took place? Our answer is that we simply have to regard that chapter as revealed Scripture. God, of course, is the only one who can tell us about the creation, and the Christian believes that God has spoken on this subject. In other words, we are coming face to face with the question of special divine revelation. What is really the question that is involved to-day? Is there such a thing as special divine revelation? The Bible says: 'He (God) made known his ways unto Moses, his acts unto the children of Israel' (Psalm 103:7). The Bible is either a revelation of God, or it is simply the gropings of the Hebrew nation and the presentation of the best that they could find. I can prove that the Christian position, the position which the Bible compels us to accept, is that this is a revelation from God. God has told us about the creation, and we believe that it is historical, that is, that it actually took place, because God has so spoken.

All this, of course, involves a proper view of God. It involves what I would call the Christian theistic position. We believe in God. We receive the Apostles' Creed: 'I believe in God the Father Almighty', and we mean what we say. On the modern viewpoint you cannot believe in such a God. But on the viewpoint of the Bible itself, that is the only God in whom we can believe. So I consider Genesis as historical and as a revelation from God.

4. The Primeval Condition of the Earth

 $\mathcal{W}$ E are told that the second verse of Genesis chapter one is a little treasure-house of mythological statements. 'The earth was without form and void'. Those two words in the Hebrew are somewhat similar in sound, and the Phoenicians, or some people at least, have preserved the concept of a god which is thought to be related to this. Others think that the concept of the abyss, the original primeval waters, suggests that there are the powers of evil. In all the creation accounts of antiquity the god has had to overcome the powers of evil. The chaotic waters, we are told, represent the evil powers, and in the Babylonian account you have the deity overcoming the power of evil. It is said that the Bible account reflects such ideas.

In the second verse of Genesis chapter one, this word *abyss* simply refers to the primeval ocean. The picture presented is of an earth covered with water, a vast deep. There was nothing evil about it. It was simply the condition in which things were at that stage. Over this deep there was a darkness. Again, the darkness does not represent something that is theologically evil, as many commentators say, for straight away God assigns a spirit to the darkness in distinction from the light.

Then again we read: 'The Spirit of God was hovering over the waters'. The Phoenicians have the concept of a world egg that split open and from it the heavens and earth formed. There are those who tell us that we should translate the words thus: 'a mighty wind was rushing over the waters', but the participle that is used here excludes that translation. It is to be translated 'hovering', and the picture is that of the Spirit of God hovering over all things as a bird hovers over its nest, so that the Spirit of God is holding all things in control. There is no reason at all why we should assume that the condition described in the second verse of Genesis chapter one is evil, why we should think that it was out of God's control, or that God was in any sense displeased with what is there presented. Rather, it is a picture of a threefold condition existing from the point of absolute creation until God says: 'Let there be light'.

Genesis and Various Cosmogonies

The question arises: What then is the relationship between the first chapter of Genesis and men's various cosmogonies or theories of creation? There are many who tell us that the Genesis account is simply a purified account of the cosmogony which the Babylonians had. When the Babylonian tablets were first discovered in the nineteenth century, a book was published called *The Babylonian Genesis*, which said that it was very clear that the account in Genesis was simply taken over from the Babylonians. In other words the Hebrew priests had brought these ideas from Babylon and written them down in Genesis one. Nowadays the view has become a little more refined, and the ideas are thought to have come into Israel through the Canaanites.

I believe that all those attempts at comparison are mistaken. If God is the Creator, and if things occurred as he tells us in the first chapter of Genesis, then God would have revealed that truth to man very early. Man would have handed that truth down to his descendants, and after the flood that truth would have been passed on to those who were not in the line of promise as well as to those who were in the line of promise. Among unbelievers we can well understand that the truth would become corrupted with superstition. Even to-day we know how rumours spread. Oral tradition in the present day is not a very reliable thing, and this has always been the case. So among those who did not believe in the true God the truth would have been corrupted by the introduction of superstitious elements. That is why in the Babylonian account we find some things that are true and others that are false. This is also the case with other cosmogonies. Elements of truth have been preserved in them, and I believe this explains the similarity between the Genesis account and the Babylonian account. Throughout the whole world there are cosmogonies containing statements and views which in themselves are true to fact. There has recently been published a book in which this question is discussed. The author is speaking of the cosmogonies of the Polynesians and the Hawaiians and others, comparing them with some of the cosmogonies that came from the ancient Near East, and in all of these there are certain elements which in themselves are reflections of the truth which God originally revealed to mankind. I believe that God chose someone to write down this material, that may have existed in written form and even in oral tradition before this time, but I believe that God used Moses to write it down and that Moses wrote as an inspired penman and was preserved from error in his writing, so that the first chapter of Genesis is a revelation from God and it towers high above any other cosmogony that comes from the ancient world. We are, therefore, to read it in the belief that what it relates is the truth.

Coming back, then, to our chapter, we find in this second verse of Genesis one, three circumstantial clauses. A circumstantial or a nominal clause in Hebrew is simply a clause that describes a condition. It does not contain action. A verbal clause contains action. 'In the beginning God created the heaven and the earth' is a verbal clause because there is action therein. The three following sentences, however, are simply descriptive. They do not contain action. 'The earth *was* desolation and waste; darkness *was* on the face of the abyss; the Spirit of God *was* hovering over the waters.' Those are descriptive clauses. Now they modify a main verb, and grammatically that main verb is given to us in the third verse: 'And God said, Let there be light, and there was light'.

5. The First, Second and Third Days

*T*HIS is the first of God's creative acts in bringing the unformed universe into the condition in which we find it to-day. Light is the foundation of all that follows, but you may have wondered why the light is mentioned without the sun. There was a time when some men said that this was a scientific error, but men do not speak that way any more. That the sun is not yet mentioned is deliberate. It is to show men that light comes from God, and that God is to be worshipped and not the sun. The ancient world was a sun-worshipping world. The Egyptian hieroglyphics speak of the god *Ra* who was the sun-god. The Hittites speak of a man that becomes a sun. In the ancient Near East the concept of the sun is very prominent. There, where the sun is shining for the greater part of the day, sinful man would lift up his eyes, see the sun in the sky, and worship it as a god. But that we may understand that light, the necessary foundation for all life, is the gift of God and not of the sun, light is mentioned before the sun. The relationship of this light to the sun I intend to leave until we discuss the work of the fourth day. At any rate, it is clear that there may be light that does not come from the sun, and I do not know that anybody says that this is an error any longer. But there is another question. God said: 'Let there be light'. What does that mean? Speech in itself is psychical, but the organs of speech are physical. That is to say, we need the mouth, tongue, lips, teeth, and so on, in order to speak, and yet speech in itself is not necessarily physical. In a dream we speak, do we not? And that is speech, yet it is not ordinary speech. So that we need not conceive of this expression in Genesis as a crude anthropomorphism. (Anthropomorphic means 'in the form of man'). Not at all! More is involved here than a mere anthropomorphism. God is infinite. We cannot circumscribe him. We are finite, and when we speak of God we can only speak from the standpoint of a finite creature. Hence all our thoughts about God, though they may be true, are nevertheless the thoughts of limited human beings. We cannot comprehend God as he is in himself. The incomprehensibility of God is a fundamental Christian doctrine. We can only think the thoughts of God which he has revealed to us. We cannot grasp him as he is. And so we speak of God using human language, and we say: 'God said'. That does not mean that he spoke in Hebrew. It does not mean that he even uttered sounds. I cannot say positively what it does mean, but I think that it does mean that there is a genuine divine speech, and that human speech is derived from divine speech. That is one of the results of our being in the image of God, that as God speaks we also can speak.

But that there is more involved here than a mere anthropomorphism, which suggests that God wills the existence of life, seems to be true by 2 Corinthians 4:6, where Paul says that God, having said that light from darkness shined forth, 'hath shined in our hearts to give the light of the knowledge of the glory of God in the face of Jesus Christ'. The King James Version reads: 'For God, who commanded the light to shine out of darkness, hath shined in our hearts'. But the original Greek would read: 'But God, having said light from darkness shined forth, hath shined in our hearts'. In other words, just as God said: 'Let there be light', so also God has shined in our hearts with the light of regeneration. 'Let the light shine forth from the darkness'. So there is a genuine divine speech, and God expresses the thought: 'Let light be, and light was'. 'And it was so'. Thus rapidly and succinctly the creation of light is stated. And God saw the light. He saw that it was good. This is the first and only place in the chapter, apart from verse thirty-one, where an object is used. 'God saw the light that it was good'. In verse thirty-one we read: 'And God saw everything that he had made, and, behold, it was very good'. In between, however, we simply have the statement: 'And God saw that it was good', with no object being mentioned. Thus you have a contrast between the condition of chaos in verse two and the cosmos given to us in verse thirty-one.

The creation of the light, then, is the first step in the removal of the condition of chaos. Step by step God is preparing the world so that man may dwell in it. He divides the light from the darkness. Notice that the word 'day' is used in verse five in two different senses. First, it distinguishes the period of light from the period of darkness. Secondly, it includes both the period of light and the period of darkness. The same Hebrew word is used in both instances. In the second chapter, verse four, we find the word 'day' used in a third sense: 'In the day of the Lord God making earth and heaven', which we might paraphrase: 'At the time when the Lord God made earth and heaven'. Then we find the phrase used in a different sense again in later scriptures—'in the latter days', or 'in that day'—where it refers to a great period of time.

One matter that Christians like to talk about is the length of these days. It is not too profitable to do so, for the simple reason that God has not revealed sufficient for us to say very much about it. The Hebrew word *yom* is much like our English word *day*, and it is capable of a great number of connotations. In itself the use of the word does not prove anything. But several matters are noteworthy. The first three days are not solar days such as we now know. The sun, moon, and stars were not in existence, at least in the form in which they are now present. That I think we are compelled to acknowledge. And the work of the third day seems to suggest that there was some process, and that what took place occurred in a period longer than twenty-four hours. I certainly believe that the framework given here is that of six days followed by a seventh. I cannot accept the so-called framework hypothesis, which maintains that there are six pictures of creation, and that they sustain no chronological relationship to one another. That is a very easy way out of the difficulty, but I think it is unsupportable. Chronology is emphasized, one day, two days, climaxing with the sixth day.

At this point we can glance at the question which

troubles all of us. How old is the earth? How old is man? It is almost universally taught nowadays that man is millions of years old, and that the earth is millions of years old. The Bible simply does not speak on the subject of the antiquity of man. That is to say, it does not give dates. And if it could be proved that some of the figures that are being used are correct, it would not affect what is stated in the first chapter of Genesis. We do well to remember that most of the scientific work of men is based on the theory of uniformitarianism, that is, that what is true now has always been true. But the fact that there have been miracles—and we believe in miracles—means that there has been an intrusion of the supernatural. I do not think we can prove anything about the antiquity of the earth, so I do not see how anybody can say that Genesis is in error at this point. We have to remember that there is a great deal that we do not know, and even the man who has not had technical scientific training must realize that scientists operate upon certain presuppositions and principles, and we have to come back to the fact that they do not come to grips with the basic question of origin. Genesis alone does that. I will come back to these matters later.

The Second and Third Days

In the second day a *firmament* is created. The word means simply an 'expanse'. It is not a material substance, but simply a separation of the waters that adhere to the earth from what is beyond. More than that we cannot say. On the third day we are told that the seas are formed, and the grass, herbs, and fruit trees grow. If I understand this aright, the beginning of the third day would show that the earth is covered with water. On that third day the oceans are formed, and the dry land appears. The word used here means 'that which is really dry', actual dry land such as fruit trees can grow in. Think of what is involved. Are we to assume that on this third day the earth emerged from the waters as a perfect sphere, smooth like a tennis ball? If the earth has been covered with water, and that is what Genesis seems to teach, would that water not affect the earth so that in the formation of the seas there would be a hollowing out process and the erection of many of the mountains? That in itself might explain many of the phenomena that are present.

Another point: Genesis mentions only those things that are necessary for man's existence. It is silent about a great many other things. For example, it mentions grass, herbs, and fruit trees, but we know that that does not exhaust the category of flora. There are many other plants that grow that are not mentioned here. Furthermore, we know that pollination is necessary for the fruit trees, but nothing is said about it. Genesis is silent on many of these questions. Later there is mention of the fish that man is to rule over, but it may very well be that God had filled these seas with life even at the earliest time, and that in this emergence of the earth from under the waters in the formation of the seas and the mountains and valleys and so on, fossil deposits were made at that very time.

There are questions that all of us have to face. Modern science, and especially popularizations of scientific works, are silent on the question of origins. They assume that the material of the earth was always present. Many adopt what is popularly called the Big Bang theory, that the material of the earth came into being or burst forth in a great explosion, the sun and moon and other bodies being involved in that also. But they do not come to grips with the origin of that material, and this is where Christianity has every right to challenge modern thought.

Men talk about the origin of the earth, but I am talking about the creation of the original material, and that is ignored in a scientific study. They tell us that that is not a matter for the scientists, that it belongs to the realm of faith or religion, or something akin to them. Not at all! It is a matter for every man to face up to. If there is a beginning, a genuine creation, then we all have this question to face, and why may it not have been that as the earth emerged from the waters much of this work of erosion was done at that time? It is quite possible that that could be the case. Then the dry land responds to the command of God and sends forth grass, herbs, and fruit trees.

6. The Fourth, Fifth and Sixth Days

*T*HERE has been progression up to this point. What God has created so far has been either inanimate, that is, not organic and without what we call life, or it has been animate and stationary, such as the grass, herbs, and fruit trees. Now we come to the work of the fourth day, and this is the place where science and Genesis are said to conflict. The sun, moon, and stars are brought into existence. Some people tell us that the Hebrew word used here simply means that God made them to appear. Evangelicals say that very often. The new edition of the Scofield Bible says so. It is a very intriguing theory, but it is not true to the meaning of the Hebrew word, and Evangelicals never gain anything for their cause by trying to force language to say what it does not say. The verb that is used here is *'asah*—God 'made'— and if you take those words just as they are, I think we shall see an answer.

There is given to us so far in Genesis a history of the development of the world. Why may there not have been a parallel development of the other heavenly bodies? In the first verse we read: 'God created the heaven and the earth', and it means just that. It does not say: 'God created the earth', but 'God created the heaven and the earth'. There may have been a parallel development of other bodies as well as of the earth. On the fourth day these other bodies are made—the sun, the moon, and the stars. It does not mean that they are created out of nothing. The material was already there. It could even be that the light that came to the earth up to this time came from one of those bodies that now is said to be the sun. I think that the fourth day means this, that God then constituted the universe as we now know it, and that would be so whether it is an expanding universe or not. If you take it that way a great deal of difficulty is removed. Genesis concentrates upon this earth. If we remember that, we shall see that we have no right to demand of Genesis what it does not claim to give us.

Notice how succinct it is, how it tells us these things in so few words, and yet says so much. The objection that is raised is that this is geo-centric, that is to say, the earth is put at the centre of things. There is a partial truth in that objection. Genesis is geo-centric. But there are two ways in which it might be geo-centric. It might be geo-centric in teaching something that was not in accordance with the facts. It might maintain, for instance, that the earth is the physical centre of the universe, and that the sun does actually rise and revolve about the earth. It does not do so. There is not one word in Genesis that is contrary to fact. It is geo-centric in another sense, in that it is discussing everything else from the standpoint of this earth. We are all geo-centric in that sense. We cannot help ourselves. We talk about 'outer space'. That is rather a modern term, is it not? Well, outer from what? What is the standard we are using for judging when we so speak? It is this earth! When the most advanced scientists of to-day talk about outer space, shall we tell them they are geo-centric, and that in consequence we are not going to listen to them? That is the way people talk about the Bible. We talk of looking up and looking down; but what is up and what is down? How else can we talk? When Paul says: 'Let not the sun go down upon your wrath', that is not an error in the Bible. What do you want Paul to say? Do you want him to go into a technical discussion of the matter? If you do that, you would forget all about the question of wrath, which is the important thing in that verse. To speak of the sun going down is not an error. It is the only way we can speak, and Genesis is geo-centric in that sense. It simply says that the great luminary, the great light-bearer, does rule the day and the night, the seasons, the years, and so on, and that is true. The sun and moon have many other functions, but they do serve this earth, and that we need to remember. What Genesis says is perfectly true to fact. Nobody can maintain that there is any error in the first chapter. There are many things that we cannot understand, but it is wrong to impute to the chapter more than it claims to give us.

The Fifth and Sixth Days

When we go on from this point we notice that there is a development, a progression in the order of statement. Again the verb *bara'* (create) is used (verse 21). God creates the great sea monsters, the birds, and the things that creep, and a blessing is pronounced upon them and the work of the fifth day. The creatures that now appear on the earth are organic and they move about. There is progression, but they are all for men. The cattle are created. Now in order to avoid redundancy of expression, the verb '*asah* (made) is used (verse 25), and the blessing is omitted, in order that the way may be prepared for the creation of man himself.

The creation of man is introduced by divine deliberation: 'Let us make man in our image, according to our likeness'. There is nothing like that in the Babylonian or other creation accounts. In the Babylonian account the god Marduk says: 'I will make men', and some commentators believe that the plural in Genesis is a deliberate rejection of the polytheistic statement of the Babylonian account. I do not think so. I think that this is intended to indicate that there is a plurality of persons in the speaker. It is not a plural of majesty. It is not God consulting his heavenly court, for in the work of salvation and in the work of creation God does not consult the heavenly court. These are the words of God alone, and it is, I repeat, an indication or an intimation that there is a plurality of persons in the speaker. It is the first adumbration of the doctrine of the Trinity that is found in the Bible. This explains the use of the plural: 'Let us make man in our image, according to our likeness'. And this idea of image and likeness is unique to the Bible.

God creates man in distinction from all that has preceded, man in the divine image and likeness. The verb *bara'* is used; so 'God created man in his own image, in the image of God created he him, male and female created he them' (verse 27). Here the uniqueness of man is set forth. Man is the crown of creation. He is supreme over all that has gone before. All that has gone before has prepared the way for man to rule the earth, and then the blessing is pronounced upon man, and God says: 'Be fruitful and multiply and fill the earth'. In the King James version it says: 'Replenish the earth', which simply means 'fill the earth'. The old English word 'replenish' simply means 'fill', but some have taken it and stressed the 're' part of it, drawing from it the conclusion that there was a pre-Adamic race. But this is certainly not a proof of anything of that nature. The Hebrew word is 'fill' the earth. In this way the blessing is pronounced upon man and the earth is set before man. Then the statement is made: 'And God saw everything that he had made and behold it was very good'. Notice, then, this progression step by step until man is created as the crown of creation.

Notice, too, that each day is designated—day one, day two, day three, day four, day five, and then *the* sixth day. With the sixth day alone the definite article is employed. This is the day of the crown of creation, the day upon which man comes from the hand of God, man in distinction from all that has gone before.

7. What about Evolution?

*T*HE question must be considered: What about evolution? This is the point, of course, where many maintain that there is a real conflict between Genesis and evolutionary theory. We are constantly being told that it is a naive view to accept what is found in the first chapter of Genesis, that this represents the cosmogony of the ancient Hebrews, and that men have seen that these things are no longer so, for they have a more advanced concept of the origin of things than was maintained in those early days. Well, is that really the case?

What is meant by evolution? Genesis uses the term 'after its kind'. The word 'kind' is a rather loose word, not to be equated with our English word 'species'. It is used perhaps as we use the English word 'kind'. It means that nothing reproduces anything that is contrary to or essentially different from itself. A man, a human being, will always reproduce a human being. A cat will always reproduce a cat, a dog a dog, and so on. This does not allow for mutations. There are mutations as we well know, and yet they are not essentially different from the parent. There may be occasional freaks, but Genesis excludes the idea that one particular plant, let us say, will produce something that is essentially different from itself. It reproduces according to its 'kind', a word that is used several times in the first chapter of Genesis.

There are those who say that the evidence for evolution is very strong. They bring up objections to the first chapter of Genesis and demand of us an explanation. Why was there light before the sun? If the days are twenty-four hours in length, how do you account for the antiquity of man? These are examples of the questions put to us. Let me say that no mere man can answer all questions to everybody's satisfaction concerning the first chapter of Genesis. It simply cannot be done, and it is foolish even to think that a person can do it. I do not like the idea of Christians always having to be on the defensive. Some almost apologize for evangelical beliefs as though they were something to be ashamed of. I think that evolution has brought its share of the difficulties and that it is time that the evolutionists began to give us some kind of an answer to the problems that arise.

At this point I want to distinguish between what I call 'atheistic evolution' and what is pretty commonly called 'theistic evolution'. The latter simply means that God used evolution as his method of creation. He changed a lower form of life into a human being—that is, he so worked that the lower form of life became a human being. But I do not believe that it is possible to hold to the Bible and to theistic evolution at the same time. By stretching things, the best that a man can do is to hold that the body of the first man evolved out of a form of life that was lower than man. You cannot hold to the evolution of the body of woman and hold to the Bible at the same time, for the simple reason that the Bible shows us how Eve was created. God caused a deep sleep to fall upon Adam, and he slept, and God took one of his ribs, and from that rib he built the woman. He brought her to the man to see what he would call her, and the man immediately recognized that she stood in a unique relationship to himself, as was not true of any of the animals. If you accept the Bible then you cannot accept the evolution of the body of woman. The best you can do, if you claim to hold to the Bible, is to hold that the body of the first man evolved from something lower than man, and, personally, I do not think that you can do even that. It is a stretching of things in the attempt to meet up to the claims of science.

The Problems of Evolution Further Considered

If theistic evolution, then, must be set aside, what do we have left? We have left what I have previously called 'atheistic evolution', the idea that an entity which was not man changed into a man. That is the fundamental point of evolution, the crux of the whole position, the idea that something which was not man became man. Now God could have caused such a change to take place, but the Bible does not permit us to believe it. So the following are questions I would ask the evolutionist who leaves God out of the picture, which is really what evolution does. First, what caused this non-man to become man? It does not help to introduce millions of years into the matter, for if you have millions of years to change right up to the point of being a man, so long as the entity is not a man the gulf between them remains tremendous. What caused that final change? That is the final question. The man has body and soul, which means that he can think and can reason. He can plan, he can conceive, and he has ability to pray to God. He has religious capacity, and if something walks around on two legs and does not have that capacity, he is not a man. Where did these abilities come from? Atheistic evolution has no answer to the question, but we have the right to demand an answer.

There is another problem involved here. If this evolution occurred, what about the origin of the sexes? You have to have a man and a woman. What caused the differentiation in the sexes? Suggested explanations have been given, but they do not explain. Very fortunately, it is supposed, one non-man became a male, another became a female. If these two became human, they mated and had children, then you can ask where those children got their wives (just as people have long enquired where Cain got his wife). The old problem arises. Probably some are supposing that at one time a lot of non-men became men. If so, what caused this to happen, and what happened to the rest who did not become men? Ah, they say, the principle of the survival of the fittest holds good. Some non-men could not do it. They could not quite make it to become men. Very well, if they could not make it at that time, they have had plenty of time to survive and become fit since then, and there are many fit animals left in the world, who are a great deal more fit than human beings are. Why does not this evolution occur to-day? If atheistic evolution is true, why cannot we ourselves somehow evolve into something better than we are? Not one of us is satisfied with what he is. Why did evolution stop?

Why do we not change into something better? We are trying to do it all the time, and yet we cannot do it. Why is it that man, the supposed crown of evolution, does things that animals would not do? I have visited the concentration camps in Hitler's Germany. They are kept there as monuments to-day, and believe me, if you go through them, you are just sickened to think that human beings could do the things that were done in those camps. Animals do not act in that way. Animals may fight for their life, but they do not act as men do. They do not plan the devilish things that fallen man plans.

God the Creator

Then you have to go back to what is most fundamental of all—how did the whole process start? The primal cell, what caused it? There is no real evidence for evolution, despite all that is being claimed. The evidence is not evidence for evolution. It is evidence of development, and that is all it is. There is no evidence to show that one entity ever has changed into something essentially different from itself. These are fundamental questions, and we have a right to expect evolutionists to answer them. The most fundamental question of all is: Where did the soul of man come from? Why is it that the highest and best animals are unable to pray? They are unable to communicate in a rational way. They are unable to do the things that man is able to do. The lowest type of man upon the face of the earth is far higher than the highest of the animals, because he has the capacity to worship God and can be brought to be a child of God, able to live to the glory of God through Jesus Christ, and that is true of none of the animals. I am not ashamed to say that I believe in the first chapter of Genesis, but I should be ashamed to say that I held to any form of evolution.

We have difficulties, we have problems, We cannot answer them all. The evolutionist has problems also. I have only touched on some of them, of course, but I want you to think these things through. When you are tempted to doubt the first chapter of Genesis, as though to believe it were something childish and naive, remember that there are problems that stare the evolutionist in the face, problems to which he has no answer.

So we have, in the first chapter of Genesis, the wonderful statement of the fact of creation in which God is exalted as the Creator. We see how step by step God brought the earth from its unfinished condition to the point where man could dwell upon it. And we see that man is the noblest work of God's creation, that all the world is before him. There is the challenge for us. There is meaning in our life. We are to go forth and live in this world for the glory of the Creator, to capture every realm of life for Christ, for it is his world. With whatever talents God has given us, and in whatever way we can, we are to show that this is God's world and that we are his creatures and that we are living erect upon this earth for God's glory.

8. Are There Two Accounts of Creation?

If you were to pick up a modern introduction to the Old Testament, you would very likely find that it maintained that in the Book of Genesis there were two accounts of creation. Some years ago a book appeared with the title *The Bible as the Word of God*. It claimed that the Bible was the Word of God, but also the word of man, and one reason for saying that it was the word of man was that there were errors in the Bible. As soon as someone begins to list those errors you know pretty well what he is going to say. He will begin by telling us that one of the first errors in the Bible is that there are two accounts of creation, one found in the first chapter, the other found in the second chapter, and these two accounts are at variance one with the other. I do not know when this rather widespread view first came into prominence. It is based upon the assumption that the Pentateuch is composed of a number of documents, one of which is the so-called priestly document P, and another is the Jehovah document J. The latter has been combined with the Elohistic document E, so you have JE. The first chapter of Genesis is said to be derived from the priestly document P, while the second chapter belongs to JE. The claim is that they represent two entirely different backgrounds and two entirely different viewpoints, and so there is an error, a contradiction, right at the very beginning of the Bible.

It seems to me that this documentary theory creates something of a psychological difficulty. If it is correct that the Pentateuch does consist of a number of documents which were finally pieced together by a redactor, then it must be acknowledged that the Pentateuch is a very remarkable work. It is not the kind of writing that very many people could produce. Undoubtedly it is one of the greatest writings in existence, and whoever was responsible for it was an artist and a genius. So if this redactor was responsible for it in its present form, whoever he was he must have been a very unusual person. But if it is so, then why did he make such a blunder at the very beginning as to put together two contradictory accounts of creation? If he was such a genius, would he not have realized that it was not very sensible to put two conflicting accounts of creation together? But until the rise of modern scholarship no one ever seems to have noticed that here were two conflicting accounts of creation. So there is the psychological problem that I think should at least be considered by those who so glibly tell us that we have two diverse accounts of creation.

Let us look at Genesis a little more closely and ask: Are there really two contradictory accounts of creation? In my view the critics who have created this redactor have created a problem far greater than any problem that the Bible itself offers. So let me ask again: Is there really a contradiction right at the beginning of the Bible? I do not think so. All we have to do is to read what the Bible actually says. When somebody tells you that there is an error in the Bible, go to the Bible and find out exactly what it says. Do not begin discussing it without reference to the Bible. When you see exactly what the Bible says, very often the 'error' disappears. So let us look at what the second chapter of Genesis says.

God's Rest

We have already noticed that the first chapter is chrono-logical, that it speaks of the creation of all things, and of God's forming the present earth so that man could dwell upon it. Then we noticed that God pronounced every-thing that he made to be very good. The early verses of chapter two next tell us that God rests, that is to say, he ceases from his labour. There is a minor point to notice in the early verses of the second chapter. The Hebrew, as also the English version, tells us that God rested on the seventh day. On that day 'God ended (finished) his work which he had made; and he rested on the seventh day from all his work which he had made' (verse 2). If you were to examine the Greek translation, known as the Septuagint, especially Codex B, you would find that it reads: 'And God finished on the sixth day his work which he had made'. That is to say, the Greek substitutes 'sixth' for 'seventh'. Now why is that? I am inclined to think that the Greek translators felt that if you render it: 'God finished his work on the seventh day', it would imply that God had worked for a while on the seventh day before ceasing his work. If I say, for example, that I finished

painting the house to-day, that means that I did some
painting to-day, and I ceased to-day. So the Greek
translators evidently reasoned that if God finished his
work on the seventh day he must have worked for a while
on that day, and then ceased. But there is no need to make
the emendation that the Greeks made. We can simply let
the Hebrew text stand as it is. The form of the verb that
is used here is often declarative, and what it means is:
And God on the seventh day declared finished the work
which he had made'. It does not say anything about his
working on the seventh day, and if the Greek translators
had known Hebrew better, they would not have made this
mistake. The verb, I repeat, is often used in this declarative manner. In Arabic you find the same usage. It occurs
in the Koran where Mohammed often says he declared
someone to be a liar—one of his favourite expressions
apparently.

Superscription or Subscription?

We move on to verse four where we find this statement:
'These are the generations of the heavens and the earth
when they were created'. And this is a key statement for
understanding the Book of Genesis, though it is mis-
understood, I think, as much as anything in the Bible.
Some people have the ability, like Humpty Dumpty in
Alice in Wonderland, to make words mean whatever they
want them to mean, and they go badly astray over verse
four. The phrase, 'These are the generations of the heavens
and the earth', is a superscription and not a subscription.
In other words, it does not bring to a close what has just
gone before. It is rather an introduction to what follows.

It is a superscription. How do I know that? The phrase occurs some ten or eleven times in the book of Genesis, and it is clear that in every one of these occurrences, that is the way in which the phrase is used. It is always used as a superscription. In fact, some scholars, followed by Moffatt in his translation of Genesis, realized that this was the case, but they said that the phrase is out of place where it stands. It should have been before the first verse of Genesis, and that is why Moffatt gets the translation: 'This is the story of how the heavens and the earth were formed when God began to create the heavens and the earth.' That is a recognition of the fact that this phrase, 'These are the generations of the heavens and the earth', is a superscription and not a subscription.

Now there are those who simply will not face up to that fact. And so, in the *Anchor Bible*, we find the phrase translated something like this: 'This is the story of how the heavens and the earth were formed', summing up what has gone before. But that is not a correct translation, and the *Anchor Bible* in its translation of Genesis is in a number of instances inaccurate. It seems to me that there is too much reading into the text very often, and this is an instance of it. The phrase does not mean 'the story' of how the heavens and the earth were formed. Let us look at it briefly. 'These are the generations'. The Hebrew word *toledoth* comes from a root which means 'to bear' or 'to beget', and it is a noun based on the causative stem of that root. It means literally: 'These are the things begotten of heaven and earth', or one might say, 'produced by heaven and earth'. A Dutch book has recently appeared on this subject—in English the title would be *Creation and*

Paradise—written by Professor Gispen of the Free University of Amsterdam. It is a very thorough, detailed analysis of the Hebrew text of the first three chapters of Genesis, and I am very happy to notice that he comes out solidly on this point, and shows that the words must be taken as a superscription. He also shows that the expression means not the story but the things produced. So what this superscription is telling us is: 'These are the things produced of heaven and earth'.

The Generations

Notice the implications of the phrase, the first being that we are not now going to read an account of creation, for that has already been given. There are, in fact, two basic divisions to the Book of Genesis. The first division is the creation. It runs from chapter one, verse one to chapter two, verse three. It is a short division. The second may be called 'The genealogies'. It runs from chapter two, verse four to the end of the Book—chapter fifty, verse twenty six. The phrase 'These are the generations of the heavens and the earth' tells us that we are not going to read further about creation, but about something that came from heaven and earth, and in particular, man, whose body comes from the created earth. Some say that the word 'heavens' spiritually suggests that the soul of man is immaterial and from the heavens. It is uncertain whether we can say that. It is a disputed point. But what is important is that we have here a statement that 'these things', that is, the things to follow, are that which was produced, or begotten, or generated, by the heavens and the earth.

Notice how that does tie up with the first chapter of

Genesis, of which the first verse says: 'In the beginning God created the heavens and the earth'. There is the origin of the heaven and the earth. God has created them. But now we are going a step further. We are no longer dealing with creation but with what the heavens and the earth which God has created have themselves produced. I think we can be thoroughly dogmatic about that. The Bible itself tells us what it is going to talk about. It does not say that this is a second account of creation. Not at all! Instead, it tells us that it is going to talk about what has come from heaven and earth. Yet the higher critics continue to repeat dogmatically, that the phrase used is a subscription. Even the *Standard Hebrew Dictionary* is in error at this point in its translation, and with reference to this word.

Take, for example, another use of the phrase in Genesis. 'These are the generations of Terah' (11:27). What follows? Do we find an account of the birth of Terah and the life of Terah? No; that has just been given. What we find is an account of that which was begotten by Terah, namely, Abraham, and the whole section that follows deals with Abraham as Terah's descendant. The same is the case with every one of the uses of this phrase in Genesis. It is very interesting to notice that, as the phrase is used, it serves to narrow down the line of promise. It begins with the broadest possible beginning, the creation of the heavens and the earth. Then the next one: 'This is the book of the generations of Adam'. It is no longer talking about animals and so on, but only of the descendants of Adam, the generations of Noah, the generations of Shem, the generations of Terah, and so on. Twice it interrupts the line of descent to speak of other lines that are not in the line of promise, and then it reverts to its main theme, which is to trace the line of descent from the very beginning down to the point where Joseph goes into Egypt. So the whole Book of Genesis has a narrowing down of reference. It begins with the widest possible conception and, step by step, narrows that down, for our interest is to read about the chosen line, how in the face of all kinds of obstacles God is fulfilling his promise that he made to the fathers. Let us realize then that this phrase, 'These are the generations of the heavens and the earth', must be a superscription, that it must introduce what follows, and it is entirely incorrect to say that it is a subscription. It therefore follows that all attempts to show that there are contradictions of the first chapter in the second chapter fall by the board.

9. Man, Woman, and the Garden

Now let us look at what follows. It is obvious that it is dealing with what comes from heaven and earth. It is particularistic. It deals with man and the placing of man in the garden of Eden, and it is a preparation for the events of the third chapter. Do not misunderstand me. I am not saying that there is no relationship with the first chapter, for that would be incorrect. The first chapter is presupposed, as is shown by the divine names, among other things. The 'Elohim God of the first chapter appears in the second chapter as Jehovah—'Elohim to show that Jehovah is the 'Elohim of the first chapter. Several things in the second chapter presuppose what has been stated in the first chapter, and surely the first chapter prepares for what follows with its constant emphasis upon 'God saw that it was good'. So the contrast stands out between the original creation and what transpires later when sin enters the world.

Verse five of the second chapter begins with a statement which is translated in rather a strange way in the King James Version, but which has been translated: 'There was no herb of the field, and no bush had yet sprouted because . . .', and then two reasons are given, 'The Lord God had not caused it to rain', and 'there was no man to till the ground'. A strange statement, is it not? Does this refer to a condition applying to the whole earth? I very much doubt it. After all, you can have things grow without rain, and you can certainly have them grow without a man being on hand. The weeds in our gardens do pretty well without our being around. Certain things will grow without the presence of man. So the very language seems to suggest something special. This is a contrast, I think, with the garden of Eden which God is about to form, and I think its purpose is to show that 'the earth is the Lord's and the fulness thereof'. But God did not place man in a barren wilderness, but in the best that this earth had. He created for him a garden, and this contrast shows what would be without that garden. It prepares us for a better understanding of the garden of Eden itself. Such is its purpose.

Now you might expect that the account would proceed to say that God caused it to rain, and that God formed man immediately. Yet it does not do that. It uses a strange word which I will give in the Hebrew. I will not use the English word 'mist'. '*Ed* is the word that occurs in the Hebrew. An '*ed* used to go up from the ground to water all the face of the ground. The term '*adamah* (ground) that is used, normally has a restrictive sense, though not always. What are we to understand by the '*ed*? Not a mist! The word is apparently related to a Sumerian word. It seems to refer to subterranean waters, and what we have here is either a breaking forth of water in some way from under the ground, or possibly a river overflowing its banks. I do not think we can be dogmatic here. So this section of ground, the '*adamah*, was watered, and the plants could grow. Thus was the first condition fulfilled by God. Next, the second condition is fulfilled. God formed man (literally 'dust') from the ground, and breathed into his nostrils the breath of life (that is, the breath that brings life), and man became a soul of life, a living soul.

Man a Living Soul

The commentators love to use the term 'anthropomorphic' when they are dealing with this second chapter of Genesis. They say: 'Here we see God acting like a potter. Just as a child takes modelling clay, so God takes the dust of the ground, or the mud, and he moulds it into the body of a man'. I think that we can very easily let our imaginations run away with us here. Does the text of Genesis actually speak after the fashion which I have just used? What it tells us is that the form of man's body was made by God. God formed man. Do we have to assume that he came down to earth, picked up actual dust in physical fingers, and modelled it as a child models modelling clay? I do not think so. How else would you express the concept in the English language, or the Hebrew language, or any other language? How else would you say that God gave to man's body a form, other than to say that he formed it? He formed it using dust taken from the ground. That is all the Bible says, and I cannot help but feel that some commentators let their imaginations run wild at this point. They make this a very naive conception, but is it so naive? How else would you state it?

CHAPTER 9

The body of man, then, is stated to come from the dust of the ground, and that statement prepares us for the statement in the third chapter of Genesis that that body will return to the dust, that the body is not all. The forming shows that God formed that body immediately, and this rules out the idea that the body of man developed from the body of some being lower than man, for God formed it from the dust of the ground there and then. But that is not all. The mere body is no longer the being. We know that when death comes we see the body before us, and that that is not the person. There is more than that. There is the divine in-breathing, and it is the divine in-breathing which constitutes the man a living soul, a soul of life. God breathes into his nostrils. Again, in what other way could we express the truth? Do we have to assume that it was a sort of artificial respiration process? I do not think so. We do not know how God breathed. That is certainly an anthropomorphic expression, but the fact is that we cannot speak about God without using anthropomorphic expressions. If you are going to use that term, and frankly I do not care for it overmuch, it means 'in the form of man'. I would rather change it to theomorphic, and say that we are in the image of God, and what we have to do is after the pattern that God has set. Yet I realize the difficulties in that. If you intend to use the term 'anthropomorphic' for expressions like this, every time you speak about God you are using anthropomorphic expressions. The first chapter of Genesis is filled with them: God saw, God said, God called, God divided, and so on. That is simply what the finite mind has to say about the infinite God, and yet Samuel R. Driver in his commentary makes much about the anthropomorphism (so-called) in this second chapter of Genesis, and so do a number of other writers. But how else would you state this beautiful truth in language that would be clearly understood? So man as body and soul comes from the hand of his Creator, man with the divine in-breathing, man who is to face the temptation that is mentioned in chapter three. Man is prepared. Also a garden is prepared that man may take care of it, for we read at once that God, having made man, planted a garden eastward in Eden.

Something appears here that I think compels us to ask about the general interpretation of this second chapter. I have been very insistent that the first chapter is to be understood chronologically. That is seen by the order of development, the progression of thought. It is seen also by the chronological emphasis—day one, day two, and so on. You do not find that in the second chapter of Genesis. There, instead of giving a chronological order of statement, the Lord is stating matters step by step to prepare for the account of the temptation. They are not necessarily given in chronological order. If you take it chronologically, first man is created; then the garden is planted; then the man is placed in the garden; then the trees of the garden grow. Can you have that garden without the trees? Then there is a description of the rivers of the garden. Then man is placed in the garden again. Now that is what you come up with if you insist on interpreting the chapter chronologically. You get the idea that God creates man. What does he do with him? Does he put him on a rock somewhere out in the desert and then form the garden and put man into it? But the garden is not yet really formed

CHAPTER 9

because now the trees grow in the garden, and then God puts man in the garden the second time. So I do not believe that the chapter was intended for a chronological interpretation.

As to this question of order of events in the Bible, we simply have to go by what the Bible itself teaches. There are certain passages in the Gospels of the New Testament which are not to be understood in chronological order. When a chapter demands chronological order then we must give it, as I think the first chapter of Genesis does. When it precludes chronological order, as I think this chapter does, then we must ask what its purpose is, and I think the purpose here is that of emphasis. If we would just remember this, we would see that there is no contradiction between chapters one and two of Genesis. The emphatic thing is the creation of man, with its constituent elements, that he may face the temptation. That is first taken care of. Next, the emphasis falls upon the garden. But this is not a complete statement about the garden: 'And the Lord God planted a garden eastward in Eden'. I think we are to understand that the garden and Eden were not co-extensive. The word 'Eden' in Hebrew may mean a delight or a pleasure. I am not sure that that is what it means here. There is a Sumerian word that means a steppe, or a plain, a wide plain, and in the eastern part of this plain God planted a garden. Without being dogmatic I give my opinion that that is what 'Eden' means. So the garden is planted.

Man the Crown of Creation

At this point we find an important lesson. God did not

just put man anywhere on the face of the globe. The theological teaching of the Scriptures here is of supreme importance. I do not think we can over-emphasize it as it runs thus: God is the Creator of the world; man is the crown of his creation: God places man in the garden. He gives to man the very best that this earth has, and man is to rule in this garden for the glory of God. Now evolutionary theory simply rules out such concepts. According to the evolutionists, man may have appeared anywhere upon this earth—it does not matter where—and in the most primitive of conditions. Man is not the crown of creation, according to the evolutionary theory. He is more or less an accident who happens to be here. We must think through what is involved in this philosophy, for it is with us to-day, and if it is true, it simply means that there is no law, there is no authority. You and I can act in any way that we like, for we are a law unto ourselves. You cannot have Christianity and an evolutionary philosophy at the same time. They are mutually exclusive. But notice the beauty that is set before us here in Genesis. Man is no accident. It is not by chance that he comes here, and God does not just put him somewhere in a cave, as the evolutionary theory would probably suppose. Instead, God puts him in a garden, a garden specially prepared for man, and in all this we see the love of God for his creatures. This fact is very important.

The Garden of God

We notice the garden again. God tells us something more about it. In it he planted trees, and these trees would mean a great deal to those who live in the Near East. You and I are accustomed to greenness and verdure, but in the Near East about the first thing you have to learn is that you have to wear sun-glasses. Trees and greenness are more or less of a rarity. Even the drab, olive tree is hardly what you would call green. But where you find an oasis in the desert—and I have seen them in the Sinai desert—the water and the greenness and the little bit of grass that is there are most welcome and most refreshing. We do not realize what a blessing water is until we have been in a desert region. So God planted trees in the garden, that is, it was the most delightful of places, the garden of God. Furthermore, these trees were for man, good for food, and a delight to the eyes. So we see that God is abundantly gracious to man.

But next we are told that there were two trees in particular, the tree of life in the midst of the garden, and the tree of the knowledge of good and evil. So step by step we are being prepared for the events narrated in the following chapter. These two trees are simply mentioned, and I think there are *two* trees. There are some who wish to translate the passage thus: 'The tree of life in the midst of the garden, even the tree of the knowledge of good and evil'. This is a possible translation, and so they get just one tree. But I think the sequel shows very clearly that two trees are intended, so that this alternative translation is not to be accepted. These trees prepare us for what is to follow in chapter three.

Next, a parenthesis is introduced, which speaks of the watering of the garden by four rivers. The Tigris and the Euphrates we are able to identify. I understand that the springs that give rise to their sources are only a few yards apart, which would seem to show the closeness of these two rivers in their place of origin. As to the other two rivers, we simply do not know what they are, and there is not much point in trying to identify them. Delitzsch in his book *Where was Paradise?* discussed the various theories as to the location of the garden of Eden. We cannot find it to-day. Even if we were within it we would not know it, for the place has changed greatly. There is a better way into the true garden of Eden for us now, that which is through the second Adam, Jesus Christ, and it is more important that we be concerned to find that Eden than to find the original Eden.

We see then that God in his abundant goodness prepared this well-watered garden for the man whom he had made. And he put him in it for a specific purpose, namely, to dress it and to keep it. What the word 'to keep it' means I really do not know. We have to think about Paradise from our fallen standpoint, and when you and I keep a garden we keep it from weeds. We keep it from animals coming in and trampling it down, and so on. Would that sort of thing have happened back in Eden? I do not think we can answer such questions. The verbs simply show that man had a responsibility, and that work is for the glory of God. We are not to be ashamed of work. Work is really a blessing. God has so made us that we have to work. We have to do our tasks, and Adam was given a task in the garden. Again, all of that is in preparation for what follows.

Now something further has to be emphasized—man is not to be alone. 'Not good', says God, 'the being of the man to his separation'. I am translating literally. 'I will make for him a help that is meet for him' (a help that corresponds to him). He needs such a help. I would say that in this brief phrase the dignity of woman is expressed as beautifully and as accurately as we can find it anywhere. Man needs that help, and to show that it is so the animals are brought before him.

Naming the Animals

We are told that God created the animals and brought them before Adam that Adam might name them. Many people think that here we are faced with a very naive and impossible conception. When I first studied Hebrew in Stanford University we had a minister who came down each week to teach that subject. For most of the time I was the only one in the class, and when he found out that I was conservative in my views he did everything that he could to overthrow my beliefs, and I can never forget how he treated this passage in Genesis. 'Now', he said, 'here is a big parade. God puts Adam out on a rock somewhere, and all the animals parade in front of him. Adam says, 'There goes a lion'; 'there goes a tiger'; 'there goes an elephant'; and so on. 'Now', he said, 'do you really believe that?' He tried to make the Scripture look as ridiculous as possible. Mark Twain has a passage in which he does something very similar. Adam comes home one night, and Eve says, 'What did you call that big animal out there?' 'Oh', he said, 'I called it an elephant'. 'Why did you call it an elephant?' 'Because it looked like an elephant'.

It is easy to make fun of the Scripture at this point, but not when you consider what is involved. And, by the way, if evolution is true, and man evolved from non-man, it involved man in the same task. Animals had to be named, and man had to do it. So before you ridicule Scripture, just realize that other proposed solutions do not get away from the difficulty. If something evolved into a man, man had to name the animals.

The idea that Adam sat on a rock and said, 'There is a lion', and 'There is a tiger', and so on, is not exactly what the Scripture tells us. In naming the animals Adam expressed their true nature. It may well be that he pronounced some sound that may have been automatically associated with an animal. Be that as it may, the narrative indicates the essential difference between man and the animals. Man named them; that is, he had the capacity to understand what they were, what their functions were, by what means they existed, how they could serve him, and so on. Adam acted as a creature created in the image of God. He could name the animals. They could not name him, but he could name them. This shows the profound difference between man and the lower creation, and it prepares us also for Genesis three, verse one, where the serpent speaks, and we realize that things are out of order.

How did Adam perform this work of naming the animals? I think simply in the way that Genesis says. God brought him into contact with the animals. It does not mean that they all paraded before him. Why may it not have been in the ordinary course of his life that he came into contact with the various animals and recognized what they were? He could classify them and categorize them and know them. I do not see anything ridiculous in that. It has been done. What is there ridiculous or naive in that conception? Genesis simply shows that because Adam understood these animals he was able to give them suitable names. He knew what they were for. Nevertheless, among them all there was not found a help that corresponded to him. The only help that corresponded to man was the woman, and her creation is related as a special work of God.

The Dignity of Woman

There is a very profound practical truth expressed in this part of Genesis, and I like to urge students preparing for the ministry of the Word to act in the following way when they enter upon their ministries. When a young couple comes before a minister with marriage in view, this part of Genesis supplies a very appropriate teaching to put before them. The woman is called a 'help' to the man, and she is 'a help that corresponds to him'. She stands before him, corresponding to him as none of the animals were, and so there is a divinely imposed subordination here. The woman is to be a help to the man, and she realizes her highest destiny when she is a help to the man. We jokingly talk very often about who is boss in the family. We should not do so. What we should aim at is the scriptural ideal. What is stated here in Genesis is exactly the same thing as the New Testament teaches. The man must be the head in the sense that Christ is the head of the church. That does not mean a boss. Sin has perverted the matter, so that, throughout the history of the world, womankind has often been degraded into a position of virtual slavery. That is wrong, and it exists in too many places to-day. Or the very opposite occurs. She takes the lead and becomes, as it were, the boss. But that does not really satisfy her, and it does not satisfy the man.

Now on this earth there will never be the proper scriptural proportions in any marriage. Sin has done its share in marring the conception of marriage. But where young people can see, before they are married, what the divine ideal is, I think it will go a long way towards avoiding unhappiness in married life. The man is to be the head of the house in this sense, that he is to know what he is going to do, that before the Lord he must have certain things he wants to do, and must do them. The wife is to be his help towards the accomplishment of that aim, and she is happiest when she plays that role of help. That is the way God has created her, and that is the way she must go. This does not mean that the husband is to be a tyrant, as some husbands are, or that he is to lord it over his wife, or be a boss. Not at all! We have seen that happen, and it brings tragedy and unhappiness when it occurs. Nor is the wife to dominate and so tyrannize over the husband that he does not dare open his mouth. When a man lets that happen, it does not speak very well for him. If the man knows what he wants to do and loves his wife, even as Christ loved the church and gave himself for it; if the wife is willing to be the help that corresponds to the husband, and they try to attain that ideal (and that involves sacrifices from both), then they come as near to having a happy marriage, I think, as can be had upon earth.

The Scripture utters a very profound truth at this point. The woman is to be a help to the man. But this is also in preparation for Genesis three, because it was through the woman that Satan entered and caused the downfall of the man. Thus the woman is created, being of the same essential nature as the man, as the animals are not. And here again this profound distinction between mankind and the animals is set forth in Genesis. There is no room for evolution here.

Finally, the chapter concludes with the statement that they were naked, the man and his wife, and they were not ashamed. So step by step this second chapter of Genesis has prepared the way for the account of the temptation that is to be given in the third chapter. See how remarkable its message is, and how we really deform it when we say that it is only another account of creation. It is not that. It has its own message, and an extremely important message at that.

10. The Fall of Man: Table, Myth or History?

WE have already seen that the second chapter of Genesis prepares the way for what is to be related in the third chapter. The two belong together intricately. In reading the second chapter we realize that step by step our minds and thoughts are being prepared for some momentous event to occur. It occurs as soon as the third chapter opens with the words: 'Now the serpent' and it gives emphasis to those words. Words that are placed first in Hebrew sentences are the emphatic words, and here 'Now the serpent' brings this animal to the fore and focuses our attention upon it.

We are told that 'the serpent was more subtle than any beast of the field which the Lord God had made'. This is a very difficult statement to understand. The word 'serpent' simply means an ordinary snake. We have no reason to read into this word anything particular. But the question arises—in what sense can we speak about a snake as being subtle? In some fables it is usually the fox that is subtle. It is always scheming and devising something, outwitting somebody, but one hardly thinks of a snake in this way. What then does Scripture mean when it tells us that the snake was the most subtle of beasts? The statement, it would seem, is made in connection with what follows, where man is tempted intellectually and in regard to his obedience to God. But we might well ask—how can a serpent be called subtle in that respect? The phrase really takes us behind the scenes, as it were, and simply points out that this serpent had the ability, as used by Satan, to tempt man. More than that we can scarcely say, but the serpent, we may notice, is created by God. It is 'more subtle than any beast of the field that the Lord God had made'. God has made other beasts, but the serpent is more subtle than these others. It speaks to the woman and says: 'Yea, hath God said, Ye shall not eat of every tree of the garden?'

Before we deal with this question we should notice the fact that the serpent speaks, and in the light of the second chapter of Genesis that is a very startling thing. We go back to the matter of Adam naming the animals. In doing so he was acting as a creature in the image of God. Only those who are in the image of God have the ability to speak and think. The animals do not have that ability. They cannot classify man as man can classify them. They cannot describe man as man can describe them. Man is not their help, but they are man's help. The Book of Genesis draws a profound distinction between the two. Man speaks, but an animal should not speak. Now here the serpent actually talks, and that would show immediately that there is something out of the ordinary. Something is wrong. Adam and Eve recognized that they alone could speak, but here an animal is speaking, and so Eve would immediately realize that something is out of order.

Is this a Fable?

There are those, of course, who dismiss this chapter as being a fable. In fables animals speak. There are several collections of fables. Aesop's is the best known, but there are other fables in which animals speak, and they form very interesting stories. You can do worse than read some of these fables. They usually have a moral, and the moral is the expression of practical wisdom. Thus, in *Aesop's Fables*, we read about a wolf and a lamb. The lamb was drinking the water downstream, and the wolf upstream. But the wolf accused the lamb of muddying the water, and that gave him an excuse to pounce upon the lamb and destroy it. The moral—that the wicked man will always find an excuse for evil-doing—is a good one. But my point is that we do not believe that a wolf ever spoke in that way, or that a lamb ever did reply. A fable is simply a story that illustrates a certain point, and when animals speak we know that that is only a literary device and nothing more than that. Is this what we have here in Genesis? When the serpent speaks are we reading something like these fables of Aesop? My answer is that we realize immediately that such is not the case. In the Old Testament animals do not speak. We have the special case of Balaam's ass, but no other cases than that and the speaking of the serpent in Genesis ever occur. Furthermore, if you are going to dismiss this as being a fable, you would have to find some kind of moral. A fable has a moral, but there is no moral attached here at all. So to say that the third chapter of Genesis is just a fable is really not to begin to do justice to it.

Is This Legend or Myth?

We know that to-day all kinds of efforts are made to deny the historicity of the events recorded here in the third chapter of Genesis, and so some would say that, though this chapter is not a fable, it ranks as a legend. All peoples have legends of one kind or another. These are more or less harmless stories that have been handed down and we are told that that is what we have here. But then, does that really satisfy us? This chapter explains the origin of sin in the world, and there is a moral earnestness about it that does not seem to fit in at all well with legend. Furthermore, the same characters that are found in the third chapter of Genesis are found also in the second chapter, and again in the fourth chapter. There is a connection here tying this all up with the entrance of sin into the world. It just does not look like the sort of story that is told for entertainment. Its moral earnestness and its seriousness do not fit at all well with an ordinary legend.

There are still stronger reasons for denying that our chapter is a legend, but I do not want to refer to them now. I want, rather, to point out that some term the chapter a myth. A myth in modern parlance is not necessarily a story about gods and goddesses. Most of us will have read stories, probably in school, about gods and goddesses, and have found them interesting, but even as children we never took them at all seriously. We did not believe that they were true. But nowadays we are told that a myth is not necessarily a story about gods and goddesses, but may be a story that presents a religious truth. In that way it differs from a fable. Also it is not simply a story about a hero or people in antiquity. A myth, they say, presents religious truth to us under the form of a story. Is this, then, what we have in our Genesis chapter? Are we dealing with a myth which does not relate something that actually happened, but simply presents religious truth to us, so that we can receive that truth and learn from it?

Is This a Parable?

Before I answer the question about myth, I want also to mention that there are some who say that the third chapter of Genesis is a parable. Here the use of the term 'parable' differs very little from their use of the term 'myth'. A parable again is a story which contains a spiritual lesson. In the New Testament there are many such parables. Our Lord used them frequently, and when he taught in parables he always applied a lesson. The disciples learned many lessons when our Lord expounded the parables to them. In the Old Testament also there are a number of parables, and they each contain a lesson. There is the story of the ewe lamb, for example. When David had committed his terrible sin the Lord sent the prophet Nathan to him. Nathan realized full well that he could not just go up to David and begin to reason with him about this sin. David was perhaps in the frame of mind where he might very well have taken the life of any person who became too inquisitive. So Nathan began by telling a story, a very simple oriental story. 'There were two men', he said, 'one rich and the other poor. The rich man had very many flocks and herds, but the poor man had nothing but one little ewe lamb which he had bought and nourished up, and it was to him as a daughter. And there came a wayfaring man, and the rich man spared to take of his own flocks and herds, but took the ewe lamb from the poor man and offered that to the traveller, the wayfaring man.' When David heard the story his heart was ablaze with indignation, and immediately he began to pass judgment. 'The man that hath done this thing shall die, and he shall restore fourfold because he hath done this thing and because he had no pity.' By that time Nathan was able to apply the lesson of the parable. He said to David: 'Thou art the man', and then he began to preach to David. He used this parable, not to entertain David, but to bring him to a confession of his own sin, so that Nathan could speak to the king and apply to him the meaning of the parable.

A parable, then, contains a lesson. Our Lord illustrated that well in the parables he taught. They contain an application, a lesson, and that, I say, is very characteristic of a parable. But you do not find that characteristic here in the third chapter of Genesis. After the account of the temptation is given, no lesson is mentioned. We are not told that we should not yield to temptation as Adam and Eve did. Nothing of that kind is given to us in Genesis. There is no lesson or application based upon the chapter. It simply recounts something which the writer believed took place, and that is the point that we have ever to keep before us.

We find remarkable support for this interpretation in the New Testament. In the fifth chapter of Romans, Paul compares the action of Adam with the action of Christ. As Adam did one thing, Christ has done another. And if all that Paul says about Adam is not true, if there was no Adam, then does it not follow that there need not be any Christ? If Adam's work is mythical, how do we know that Christ's work is not mythical? If Adam is not a historical character, then it is not necessary to believe that Christ is a historical character. That is the whole thrust of Paul's argument. Any of the verses that he uses in that fifth chapter, beginning at verse twelve, would illustrate the point: 'Wherefore, as by one man . . .' Take verse eighteen as an example: 'Wherefore as by the transgression of one man it is unto all men to condemnation, so also by the righteous act of one man it is unto all men unto justification of life'. That is one of the most profound statements in Scripture. Notice what is involved there. 'Wherefore', as an introductory word, connects the two parts of the verse—just as this is true, so this is also true. That is what Paul is saying: 'As by the transgression of one man (that is, Adam) it is unto all men to condemnation'. In other words, Paul is saying that the reason why all men are under condemnation stems from the fact of the first man, Adam.[1] Then he brings in a conclusion: '. . . so by the righteous act of one'—that is, our Lord's death and resurrection—'it is unto all men unto a justification that results in life'. The righteous act of the Lord corresponds to the transgression of Adam. What Paul is saying is that the justification which Christians receive is based upon the righteous act of Jesus Christ, and that righteous act of Jesus Christ is compared with the transgression of the first man. There are two men who represent the human race. The first man is of the earth, earthy. The second man

1. For further comment on this see Appendix.

is the Lord from heaven. If the first man is mythical and never lived, then the whole argument regarding the second man is worthless. Note well the significance of all this. Paul believed in the historicity of Adam, and inasmuch as Romans is the Scripture, we may trust what he has to say in the matter. So we cannot simply dismiss Adam as a non-historical figure.

11. The Fall of Man: Its Main Characteristics

ANOTHER explanation of Genesis chapter three is frequently proposed. We are told that it represents the experience of every man. Adam is every man, and every man is Adam. And to support that view the idea is brought forth that the Hebrew word *Adam* simply means mankind. You are Adam, and I am Adam. Every man is Adam. What can we say about that? We are told that Adam's experience is our experience, that this chapter is given to us to warn us about the pitfalls of temptation. We meet with temptations that we must fight, that we must resist, and if we will read about Adam we shall realize the tragedy of yielding to temptation. Such, we are told, is the meaning of the passage.

Let us look at the chapter more closely to find out whether this teaching is really true. Is it true that Adam's experience is that of every man? It is not true at all! Adam's experience is not our experience. Adam is the only one who passed through that experience. When he was faced with temptation he was an innocent creature, and by yielding to temptation he became a sinner. You and I, by yielding to temptation, do not become sinners. We are sinners already. We do not fall into a state of sin and misery. We are born into a state of sin and misery. As fallen creatures we yield to temptation, and by so doing we become hardened in our sin. But we do not become sinners by yielding to temptation, by sinning. Adam became a sinner by sinning. We are already sinners. Adam fell through his act. We are already fallen. Hence there is a profound difference between Adam's case and our own. Adam's experience is not the experience of every man. It was a unique experience. Adam and Eve were the only ones that passed through that experience. So it will not do to say that Adam is every man, and that his experiences are our experiences. The matter is far more serious than that.

The Only Account of the Origin of Sin

I next call your attention to the further fact that the third chapter of Genesis is the only writing in the world which accounts for the origin of sin and misery in the world. In the Babylonian creation account there is nothing corresponding to a fall. Rather, the gods themselves right from the start are bad actors. In none of the documents of antiquity outside Scripture is there an account of a fall. Take Ovid's *Metamorphoses* as perhaps the best example that can be chosen. Ovid explains that there was a time when everything was fine. All went well for man. There was no sickness; people did not cheat one another; it was a sort of political Utopia. God is not brought into the picture, but all went pretty well for man. Then suddenly things changed. There was sickness. There was cheating, and so on. And that is the closest, so far as I know, that you can come to the third chapter of Genesis. But the *Metamorphoses* do not give anything like an explanation of the change of which they speak. There is nothing that is parallel to the account of a fall, nothing that explains the true nature of what happened to man.

The condition in which we find ourselves to-day is not simply one of unhappiness, not merely one in which there is sickness, in which people cheat one another, and so on. It is far more serious than that. According to the Bible we are in a fallen state in which our heart is corrupt. And not only is our heart corrupt, but we are guilty before God, and we can do nothing to deliver ourselves. The only thing that can be done must be done by God himself, and God has done it. What the Bible tells us is unique. In other words, you simply cannot take this third chapter of Genesis and say that it is one of a number of similar accounts. It is not. It is a unique account. There is no parallel to it anywhere in the world. Other cosmogonies do not even come to grips with the problems that are involved, for they do not see what those problems are. I say again, Genesis three is unique. We keep on saying so. Adam's experience is not the experience of every man.

When we look at the remainder of the Bible we realize that this chapter purports to relate to us what actually took place. That does not mean that there is no symbolism in the chapter. There is symbolism, but we must interpret it aright, especially with regard to the trees of the garden. They have a symbolical meaning, but that does not mean that they were not real trees. In a certain sense Adam, as the representative of the human race, has a particular significance, but that does not mean that there was no Adam. Our Lord quoted from the Book of Genesis. The New Testament refers to it. It is perfectly clear that the New Testament regards it as that which has actually happened. So the serpent speaks. We cannot dismiss this as a mere fable, and I have brought in all these other views to get rid of them in one breath. They simply do not help us to understand the third chapter of Genesis.

The Language of the Serpent Deceptive

The language of the serpent is deceptive. The Hebrew particle can be rendered something like this: 'Yea, hath God said ye shall not eat of the fruit of the trees of the garden?' You can almost hear the tone of voice that was used. It was to imply that God was very niggardly, that he was withholding from Adam and Eve something that would have been for their good. 'Has God really said this, that you must not eat of the fruit of the trees of the garden? What a mean thing that is!' Thus we read and hear the way that Satan approaches. Then Eve replies to him: 'Of the fruit of the trees of the garden we may eat, but of the fruit of the tree that is in the midst of the garden, God has said, Ye shall not eat of it, neither shall ye touch it, lest ye die'. It may be that Eve's intentions were well meant, but she is not accurate in her reply. First of all, she generalizes it. She uses the plural instead of the singular. God had said to Adam: 'In the day that *thou* eatest thereof, dying thou shalt surely die'. Eve uses 'ye' not 'thou', making it general and plural. Furthermore, she uses another word, saying: 'Ye shall not eat of it, neither shall ye *touch* it, lest ye die'. The word 'touch' here probably means more than just handling the fruit. It is probably a synonym for eating of the fruit. But in any case, it is an addition to the command of God.

Whether Eve was merely interpreting the command, or whether she was guilty of inaccuracy may be a question for dispute. I am inclined to think that the latter is the case, because she has given the Evil One the opportunity that he wants. There is a lesson for us at this point. Do not try to reason with Satan. I do not mean that Satan is going to appear to you and sit down to talk things over. Not at all! I do not think that when Martin Luther threw the inkpot at the Devil he hit the Devil. But I think he hit the Devil not so much with that inkpot as with the things that he wrote and preached. The Devil was spending, I think, an undue amount of time with Martin Luther, which means that Luther was being faithful to Christ. The reason why the Devil lets most of us go by without bothering too much about us is that we are not causing him enough trouble. But when we are faithful to Christ then the Devil becomes very much concerned. When I say that we should not talk things over with the Devil, or reason with the Devil, I would simply call to your mind what our Lord did. When evil is presented to us, do not try to rationalize that evil, but simply remember the Scripture: 'It is written', 'Thou shalt not', and so on. The only way to handle evil of any kind is to appeal to the Scripture, and if we do that temptation and the tempter will flee from us.

I am inclined to think that Eve slipped up here. She should have realized immediately that something was wrong. As I have said already, she should have realized that serpents cannot speak. But she reasoned with it, and that gave Satan his opportunity, and he came right out and said 'Ye shall not surely die'. His language is almost vicious in its forcefulness. In the Hebrew it would be read: 'No'. 'No' is the first word that he thunders out—'No'. The idea is that this thought that they would die is just not true. The English: 'Ye shall not surely die' is rather weak. The Hebrew reads: 'No, ye shall not die', meaning: 'The statement of God is not true. Ye shall not surely die'. Thus Eve is placed in the position of choosing between God and Satan.

Do you think that Eve was a neutral, weighing the claims of God on the one hand, and the claims of the Evil One on the other hand? I do not think so for a minute. I think she was on the side of the Devil or she would never have listened to the serpent. There is no such thing as neutrality. We are either for Christ or against Christ. Nevertheless there is a problem here, a very serious problem. It is one that we cannot solve, but if we can recognize its existence, we have gone a long way to understanding it.

Freedom of Choice

Adam and Eve were left to the freedom of their will. They were not forced from without to do evil. That, I think, we can surely say. Satan had no power to compel them to sin. Their choice was a choice of free volition. They chose to do evil.

Let us go behind the scene and probe more deeply into the question. A being chooses in accordance with its nature. Let me illustrate that with respect to God. The Bible says that God cannot lie. To lie would be contrary to God's nature. God cannot deny himself. He cannot go contrary to his nature. He cannot lie. He cannot do evil. If you wish to say that this is a limitation, very well, but it is a blessed limitation. Our Lord could not have yielded to the Evil One. There is a problem here. You may say: 'How then could he have been tempted?' I cannot answer that question. All I know is that the Bible shows us a very real temptation, and yet we know that our Lord remained sinless. The possibility of his sinning is not to be contemplated.

Adam and Eve were created good. 'God saw all that he had made, and behold it was very good'. The question then is: How could sin find lodgment in a soul that was good? How could the change in nature have taken place? Let me illustrate this by the case of regeneration. We know that when a man is dead in trespasses and sins, when he is an unbeliever, he simply does not have the power to come to Christ. He is dead, and a dead being cannot act like a living being. There is very much evangelism to-day that denies this. For example, I have heard men say at young people's conferences: 'God has done everything he can do to save you. Now his hands, as it were, are tied, and it is up to you.' I answer that if it is up to us, we are lost, for we simply have not got the power to change ourselves. We cannot come to God in our own strength. We are lost, fallen creatures, and it requires the sovereign power of the Spirit of God to bring us to newness of life. 'Ye must be born again', says our Lord, but we can no more cause our own new birth than we could cause our physical birth. As we were passive in our first birth, so are we passive in the new birth. We cannot cause ourselves to be born again.

The way that the Spirit of God operates is very wonderful. He commands us to preach the gospel, and in preaching the gospel we command men: 'Believe on the Lord Jesus Christ and thou shalt be saved'. But there is no magic in those words. I preach those words, but in themselves they can do nothing. But the Spirit of God in mysterious fashion causes the soul who hears these words to be born again, and the first conscious logical act of the new-born soul is to believe on Jesus Christ. If any ask: 'Am I born again?', I reply: 'Do you believe on the Lord Jesus Christ? Do you trust him as your Saviour?' If you are trusting Christ for salvation, then you are born again, for no man who is yet in his sins can trust Christ for salvation. We cannot act contrary to our nature, and if my nature is a fallen nature, then I am at enmity with God. I hate God. I hate his words. I hate all that he stands for. And it is only when God himself has opened the eyes of my understanding through regeneration that 'old things are passed away; behold, all things are become new'. Now I love God, his word, his people, and his work. But as long as I am in my fallen state I will never come to Christ. I know that there is mystery here, but I know this, that no man has ever saved another man, or can save him. It is the Spirit of God alone who can bring a fallen soul to newness of life, who can regenerate it, who can change the nature.

Dwight L. Moody met a man who was lying in the gutter intoxicated, and the man said to him: 'I am one of your converts'. Moody said something like this: 'Yes, I guess you are one of my converts. If you were the convert of the Holy Spirit you would not be where you are now'. This illustrates my point. Man cannot save man. We cannot save ourselves. We cannot change our nature any more than the leopard can change his spots. We cannot do it. It requires sovereign grace. It is God alone who gives us the new nature, and once we have it, then our heart's affections are entirely different from what they were before.

12. The Fall of Man: Its Accompaniments

*T*o come back to Genesis—What caused the change in the nature of Adam and Eve? If Eve yielded to the Devil she must have been a fallen creature, and Adam also, as he copied her position. But what caused the change? The theologians use certain Latin phrases about the matter. They mean 'able to sin' and 'able not to sin', and so on. And that sounds very learned, but it does not explain anything. And if, when you are preaching, you use the Latin phrases too, it may sound as if you knew what you are talking about, but it does not explain a thing. We cannot explain it. We do not know how sin could find a lodgment in a human soul that was good. So we simply cannot explain the change that came about in the nature of the first human pair, but it must have taken place.

Another question, perhaps of less significance, is: When precisely did the change occur? Did it occur at the instant when the Evil One spoke to Eve, and she responded to him? Personally I am inclined to think so. But again it is impossible to be positive. Yet I fear that when the serpent said: 'Ye shall not surely die', he was talking to a person who was already on his side.

Satan's Deception

Notice what a remarkable psychological study this is of the way in which Satan acts. When he said: 'Ye shall not surely die', he comes right out with what you might call a good honest lie, if you could call it that. A straightforward lie like that usually does not do a great deal of harm. If you find that a man lies, you soon catch on, and you have no more dealings with him. The little child, for example, who has been told not to eat any of the candy, and gets it over her face, and then says to her mother: 'I did not take any', is not deceiving her mother. She has told a straightforward lie, and it has not deceived the hearer. Satan uses that kind of lie whenever it suits his purpose. But there is a far more effective way of deceiving than that, namely, to impugn the motives of someone else. He sees that Eve is listening to him, and so he goes on to say: 'For God knows that in the day that ye eat thereof, your eyes will be opened, and ye shall be as God, knowing good and evil'. There is Satan's reason. He is hitting below the belt, as it were. Satan works in that way. I do not think we can make a greater mistake than to assume that Satan comes with an objective argument.

Think of what often happens in the churches in these days. We have controversy every now and then. We must needs have it, because it is the truth of God that is involved. But the tragedy of it all is that the doctrines in dispute cannot be brought out into the open and discussed objectively. There is always someone who introduces personalities and impugns the motives of the man who is taking a different position. One of the greatest experiences of my life has been my association with the faculty of my seminary. We do not always see eye to eye on everything, on matters of detail, but we have been able to discuss matters, each one presenting what he thinks to be right, and then to go out to lunch together as though there had never been any difference of opinion. I think the reason for that is that everyone is sincerely trying to say the thing that he believes to be right, and so we can go on in a friendly spirit. We have the same thing in our presbytery, and I am grateful for it. We do have differences of opinion, but they have not broken personal friendships, because each man is trying to say the thing that he believes is right. We must have honest discussion in the church. Failing that, the church is going to die. We have to be constantly considering the things of God, and we must expect differences of opinion. When you have that kind of controversy it can be carried on in love. We can respect one another, even though at times we may disagree with one another. We find that out as we go on. The same holds true of denominations. They do not agree on everything, but the remarkable thing to me has been that we can respect one another's differences. We can differ in love, and we can realize that other people are good Christian people, even though we may not quite see everything as they do. We need to have that respect for one another which is based upon genuine Christian love, and which allows other people to have honest differences of opinion from yourself. When Christians can get along in that way, we have real Christian unity. I think that

Christian unity is a fact. We see it wherever Christian people get together. When there are differences they are discussed in love, and we realize that each one is in earnest in trying to understand the Scriptures. There is real Christian unity because it is based on Christian love. But that is not the way the Devil fights, and we find very often that those who are on the side of the Devil use his tactics.

One of the greatest disgraces of the church of Christ—and this applies to the Protestant churches as well as to the Roman Catholic church—is the playing of politics in the church by ecclesiastical politicians. That type of person speaks whatever will gain the end that he desires. You can see it happening in church history. The burning of John Huss, for example, will serve to show what I have in mind. People will manoeuvre behind the scenes in order to suppress their opponents. It has been vividly brought home to me by the experiences I had in connection with the late Dr. J. Gresham Machen. Nobody would come right out in the open and answer his arguments, but they could smear his name. They could spread stories about him that were not true, and those stories are hard to live down. People are willing to believe the falsehood rather than the truth, and this is the way that Satan fights. Here is a good practical rule for us as Christians: when somebody says something derogatory to you about someone else, just forget it. Do not believe it. It may be true; it may not be true. Whatever you do, do not spread it; do not repeat it. Gossip is a terrible thing. At times I think it one of the worst of sins. You can destroy a person's character by gossip, and Satan delights in that. This gossip simply eats the bones of another person and destroys him. It is easy to spread derogatory stories about a minister who is contending for the truth, because they take hold and they do a great deal of harm. You may for a time effectively stifle his witness, but if that man is contending for the truth earnestly, remember that the truth has a way of coming to the fore sooner or later. It is wonderful how God defends those who are on his side. Truth will prevail in the end. We must help those who are defending the truth by refusing to believe the stories that Satan spreads about them. All kinds of stories were spread about the late Dr. Machen. There was no truth in them, but people believed them. I say these things because in Genesis chapter three that is precisely the line that Satan is taking: 'God knows that in the day ye eat thereof your eyes will be opened'.

Their Eyes Were Opened

What Satan says is particularly damaging because formally it is true. The Scripture says: 'Their eyes were opened'. It was an opening of the eyes, though not of the kind that Satan had in mind. 'Your eyes will be opened, and ye will be as gods, knowing good and evil'. Formally, yes! God knows good and evil. God loves the good, because good is the expression of his nature. God hates the evil, because the evil is contrary to his nature. But Adam and Eve would know good and evil also. They would know it from the standpoint of fallen creatures. They would love the evil and reject the good. That is what would happen, but Satan does not say so. By this formally true statement he impugns the motives of God and he deceives Eve. He implies that God is somehow withholding something good from them: 'Ye will be as gods, knowing good and evil'. The implication is that God does not want man to have what *he* possesses. In other words he is jealous. That was a vicious thing to do, and that is still the way in which Satan fights. It lies behind so many of the theologies and philosophies that hold out to man that he can have anything that he wants if only he will abandon orthodox Christianity and take their new views of life. That is what Satan is doing to-day.

One thing about Satan must be said, and that is that he is not very original. He is presenting to-day the same kind of lie that he presented to Eve in the garden of Eden. The new morality is the very thing that he offered her. What he is saying in effect is this: 'Eve, do not listen to law. Authority deadens. Love is the law of life, so express yourself, and if you would be a free person and not bound by tradition and authority, eat of the forbidden fruit and be as gods, knowing good and evil'. It is the same line that Satan uses to-day, and the new morality and the new theology are nothing different from what is found in germ, and offered to Eve, in the garden of Eden.

So Eve responds. Listening to the lie, she looks at the tree and sees that it is a delight to the eyes and good for food. But she looks at it now from the standpoint of one who is on Satan's side. She partakes of the fruit, she gives to her husband, and he eats also. Someone may ask: 'Where was Adam all the time?' The Bible does not tell us. I assume he was present there, because she gave the fruit to him: 'her husband was with her'. More we cannot say for the simple reason that the Bible does not say more.

But now we are told that their eyes were opened, and

so what Satan had said came formally true. They were opened, however, not to the delights that Satan had promised them. Their eyes were opened now to their true condition, or perhaps it would be more accurate to say that their eyes were opened to the consequences of their condition, and they realized those consequences in the presence of shame. They realized that now they were naked, and they misrepresented nakedness and sought to cover it up. Before, they had not been ashamed. Before, they had judged all things from a right principle, and from the standpoint of God's revelation. Now they judge everything from the standpoint of a fallen human being, and, consequently, from now on Adam and Eve are basically mistaken in all that they say, in all that they think. Thus they seek to cover up their shame, their nakedness, and this is the first of man's many tragic acts to alleviate the situation in which he finds himself. This is the first attempt at salvation by human works. This is the first attempt to better the world in which fallen man finds himself, to use the means that are at his disposal in order to alleviate conditions. So they make a covering for themselves. But then, of course, this is not satisfactory.

Sin Involves Guilt

There is brought home to us here very clearly the nature of man's fallen condition. Sin involves first of all a corruption of the human heart, and that is seen in the shame that Adam and Eve feel here. 'The heart is deceitful above all things and desperately wicked. Who can know it?' (Jeremiah 17:9). This is the first thing that sin involves, and the heart has to be changed before there can be any entrance into heaven, and before there can be any reception into the presence of God. Man's heart has to be changed, and it is only God himself who can give to man a new heart. If that were all, that would be tragic enough. But there is more involved.

Sin involves not only pollution of the heart, but guilt before God. Hence, when Adam and Eve 'hear the voice of the Lord God walking in the garden in the cool of the day' (verse eight) they hide themselves. They cannot face God any more. Sin involves guilt before God, and when we say that a soul is guilty, we mean that he is blameworthy and liable to punishment. Fallen man not only has a corrupt heart, but he is guilty before God and cannot stand before him. I state this emphatically because we are living in a day when the doctrine of universalism is being revived with tremendous force. It is not being called universalism, but we are being told that all men are already reconciled to God, and all they need is to realize that they are reconciled to God. All men will be saved. No man will be lost. And, as one theologian said recently, 'I do not know of anybody that is actually in hell'. That is the tenor of the present day, that all men will ultimately be received by God. But that is not what the Bible teaches. Sin involves guilt before God, and the guilty sinner cannot stand in God's presence. Let us thank God that there is a deliverance, a deliverance both from the power of sin and from the guilt of sin. And that deliverance is found in the obedient work of the Second Adam, who is our Lord Jesus Christ.

13. The First Messianic Prophecy

THE third chapter of Genesis works up to its climax in the promise that is given in verse fifteen, where the Lord speaks to the serpent. We have already seen that the sin in which Adam and Eve engaged involved a corruption of their hearts and also guilt before God. They could not face God when they heard his voice in the garden, and so the Lord in loving fashion, by means of questions, brings out their true condition. And then the chapter really climaxes in verse fifteen. We notice that there is first of all the divine initiative: 'I will put enmity'. It is not an encouragement or an exhortation to man to be at enmity with the serpent, but rather the divine initiative. Salvation is always of grace, which means simply that it is of God, and had not God taken the initiative here, there would have been no salvation.

Secondly, we notice that the salvation or deliverance consists in the reversion of attitude on the part of the woman: 'Enmity will I place between thee and the woman, and between thy seed and her seed'. This means that the woman had to learn that the serpent was her enemy and that God was her friend. It does not imply that there has to be a reversion of attitude on the part of the serpent, because the serpent was really the enemy of mankind all along, although he appeared as a friend, and although he gave the impression to Eve that he was doing something that would be a benefit to her. Actually he was her enemy, seeking the destruction of her soul. So there does not have to be any change on the part of the Evil One, but man must see that the serpent is not his friend. This simply means that there must be a complete reversal of attitude that is brought about by God himself. I think this comes very close to the New Testament doctrine of the New Birth. The unbeliever, the man who is yet in his sins, is the enemy of God. He is not a disinterested person. He hates God and he hates God's ways, and he needs a reversal of attitude such as only God can give him.

In the third place, we notice that this enmity extends to the respective seeds. 'Enmity will I place between thee and the woman, and between thy seed and her seed', that is, between the descendants of Satan on the one hand and the descendants of Eve on the other. But what is meant by the 'seed of Satan'? I am inclined to think that it refers to evil men, men who throughout the course of history have aligned themselves on his side as over against God, so that even here there is an intimation that in the world there will be two kinds of people, those who are with God and those who are against God. This enmity extends between their respective seeds. It may be, however, that the word is broader than that. There is a kingdom of evil over which Satan rules. Included in it are demons, fallen angels, all who would do the will of Satan in opposition to God.

In the next place, we notice that the enmity will culminate in a decisive blow being struck which destroys the serpent. Let me quote the verse literally: 'He shall bruise thee as to the head, and thou shalt bruise him as to the heel'. Thus the promise is given that somehow from the human race there will arise One who will deliver the blow that will destroy the serpent. This is the first Messianic promise in the Old Testament. It is the fountain from which all the others flow. It is given to us in very broad and general terms, and from this time on, as time progresses, the Lord reveals more and more detail concerning the Messiah who is to come. I think we are warranted in regarding this as a genuine Messianic prophecy. It points forward, saying that the seed of the woman, a human being, will give that fatal blow which will destroy the serpent and set man free from his power.

Adam responds to this in faith. He calls his wife's name Eve, for she is the mother of all living. The word 'Eve' in the Hebrew is a very interesting word. Nouns in the Hebrew which are built on that formation are nouns which indicate that a person is something habitually or regularly. So Eve is she who indeed gives life. Adam responds in faith to the promise of God and acknowledges that from his wife life will come. He believes the promise that God has given, and in response to that faith of Adam, God clothes the man and his wife.

The Tree of Life

The Lord is concerned that the man should not partake of the tree of life. I want to say a little about the tree. In the first place, I do not think that the tree of life or the tree of the knowledge of good and evil had any magical properties. There was nothing in the fruit of the latter tree that in itself would harm anybody. We do not know what kind of a tree it was. The tradition that it was an apple comes from a misunderstanding. The Latin word for 'apple' (mālum) resembles the Latin word for 'evil' (mălum), and somebody somewhere misinterpreted the word, taking it to mean 'an apple', and so the idea came in. But there is nothing in the Hebrew to support it.

The tree of the knowledge of good and evil had, however, a sacramental significance, that is to say, if one partook of the fruit of this tree when God had forbidden it, then one was disobeying God, and the sin consisted in disobeying God. I once read a book which endeavoured to harmonize the Bible and science. In the course of his discussion the author said that the fruit of the tree contained within it the seeds of old age, so that if a man ate of this fruit he would grow old. I think the writer misunderstands the whole situation, for his words imply that the fruit had a certain magical power, and that is not at all what the Bible teaches. It was not the fruit itself, that could produce harm, but it was the fact of disobeying God that produced the harm. God had set forth this tree as a test of whether the man loved him or not. If man loved him he would abstain from this tree, but if he did not love him he would disobey him. He would eat of the fruit of the tree, and that is what man did. Hence, death came into the world. Man disobeyed God. When it says: 'In the day that thou eatest thereof thou shalt surely die', that was fulfilled. This death is a spiritual death.

You might say that the seeds of death were within man

as they are within us now, and that these seeds ripen and mature, and then, when they do so, physical death results. I do not think we have to maintain that Adam died physically on that particular day, but at the same time he was dead as soon as he ate that fruit. He was in death, and it would only be a matter of time until physical death claimed him. And he would be separated from God for ever unless God delivered him from that condition, as God actually did. But now in this condition he is not to partake of the tree of life. The Lord says: 'Lest the man stretch forth his hand and partake of the tree of life and live for ever'—and then the sentence is broken off. The apostle Paul used this type of writing very often. He begins a sentence and then he breaks it off in the middle, he is so strongly worked up with his argument. And here we have that same construction. 'And now, lest he stretch forth his hand and take of the tree of life and live for ever'—and then you expect a conclusion, 'I will drive him from the garden', or something like that—but the conclusion is not stated.

Why is there a concern on the Lord's part that the man should not eat of the fruit of the tree of life? We cannot answer this question in a dogmatic way, but I simply make this suggestion. If the man had eaten of this tree he would have eaten of it when he had no right to do so. No man can eat of the fruit of the tree of life unless he has the right thereto. Had Adam eaten of this tree when he had not the right thereto, he would have been doing a sinful thing, and I suppose he would have been confirmed in a state of sin in which he would have existed for ever, and from which there would have been no deliverance. I cannot prove this, of course, but I rather think that is what is intended. The New Testament makes it clear to us that no man is to partake of the tree of life until he has the right to do so, and there must come the second Adam, who by his obedience (as the first Adam disobeyed) obtains for his people the right to partake of the tree of life. We will eat of that tree when we have the right to partake of it, and that right we receive through Christ. Such is the way in which this third chapter of Genesis closes.

Appendix: God's Covenant with Adam[1]

In Chapter VII of the Westminster Confession of Faith there are six sections devoted to 'God's Covenant with Man'. In its second paragraph the Confession speaks of the covenant of works: 'The first covenant made with man,' it asserts, 'was a covenant of works, wherein life was promised to Adam; and in him to his posterity, upon condition of perfect and personal obedience.' In characterizing God's prohibition to man, mentioned in Genesis 2, as a 'covenant of works,' the Confession is employing familiar and often-used terminology. Is this prohibition of Genesis 2, it may be asked, accurately characterized by the term 'covenant', and if the term 'covenant' is satisfactory, may we properly denominate it 'the covenant of works'?

Whatever be our reaction to this question, there can be no doubt that the Confession does accurately describe what happened in Genesis 2. The initiative is very

1. The following extract has been added by the present publishers. It is taken from the chapter by E. J. Young entitled 'Confession and Covenant' in *Scripture and Confession*, A Book about Confessions Old and New, edited by John H. Skilton, Presbyterian and Reformed Publishing Co., 1973.

definitely ascribed to God, for the Confession speaks of a covenant 'made with man.' Furthermore, the Confession in agreement with Scripture states that life was 'promised to Adam.' At this point, however, objection may be raised and the question asked, 'Did God promise life to Adam upon condition of perfect obedience?' Such a promise is not explicitly recorded, and hence it might be maintained that it was never made.

To evaluate properly the situation, therefore, we must consider the passage in Genesis. In Genesis 2:17 God declares to Adam that 'from the tree of the knowledge of good and evil thou mayest not eat, for in the day of thy eating from it thou wilt surely die.' Were one to read merely this verse he might well receive the impression that the prohibition had reference to Adam alone. That such was not the case, however, is seen in the fact that the scriptural sequel teaches that not only Adam but also all men descended from him by ordinary generation have died and do die. When one turns to the fifth chapter of Genesis, he notes the repetition of the refrain 'and he died.' In the midst of the genealogy of the chosen line, the seed of life, there is death, for death forms the background against which this fifth chapter is written. Only in connection with Enoch is the phrase omitted. With all of the others in the chosen line, however, there appears this striking reminder of the Lord's declaration, 'thou shalt surely die,' and also of the serpent's falsehood, 'ye shall not die.'

How are we to explain this insistence upon the continuous hold of death on mankind? That the Book of Genesis would explain it as due to the transgression of

Adam is apparent. It is only thus that one can properly understand the promise given in Genesis 3:15. This promise loses its force if the descendants of Adam are not to die. It is of meaning only when we realize that it is a promise to men who have fallen into sin. From mankind, according to this verse, there will arise the woman's seed, who will deliver a capital blow against the serpent and who in turn will himself be bruised on his heel. The enmity that God is to place between the serpent and the woman is one that will extend to their respective seeds. The descendants of the woman are descendants of a woman who has fallen from the estate wherein she was created into an estate of sin and misery. It would appear, then, even from this consideration, that Genesis does teach that when Adam transgressed, not only did he himself die but also all his posterity who by ordinary generation were descended from him.

This fact supports the statement made by A. A. Hodge in his Commentary on the Westminster Confession of Faith, 'In the first covenant that concerned mankind God dealt with Adam as the representative of all his descendants.'[1] And herein is an important characteristic of the biblical covenant. It is true that this characteristic is not found in all the biblical covenants, but it is indeed found in some of them. In the Abrahamic covenant, for example, we read: 'I will make of thee a great nation' (Gen. 12:2a); 'to thy descendants I give this land' (Gen. 15:18a). In Genesis 17 this aspect also receives stress: 'And I shall give my covenant between me and thee, and I shall

1. A. A. Hodge, *A Commentary on the Confession of Faith* (London, 1870), p. 120.

multiply thee exceedingly exceedingly' (17:2); 'I, behold! My covenant is with thee, and thou shalt become the father of a multitude of nations' (17:4); 'And I shall establish my covenant between me and thee and between thy seed after thee for their generations for a covenant of eternity, to be to thee a God and to thy seed after thee' (17:7).

When we turn again to Genesis 2 we note that it is God who presents to Adam the prohibition and the administration of the prohibition. It is not a mutual pact or agreement entered into by God and Adam as partners on the same level, but rather a divine initiation. This is an essential element of the biblical covenant that God makes with man, and on the basis of the appearance of this element alone it would seem that there is justification, even though the technical terminology of the covenant is not employed and the word for covenant is not found, for regarding this divine administration as partaking of the nature of what elsewhere is denominated by the term 'covenant.'

Is the Confession, however, justified in its assertion, 'Wherein life was promised to Adam, and in him to his posterity, upon condition of perfect and personal obedience'? A superficial glance at Genesis might give the impression that the Confession has here gone beyond the legitimate sphere of exegetical investigation and is simply setting forth a position of questionable scriptural support. In answer to such an objection, we must again examine the language of Genesis. It is apparent that the words in which God addresses Adam express a prohibition. It declares to Adam what he is not to do. Such negative language might at first sight appear not to be instructive, but this is not the case. If the penalty for disobedience was everlasting death, it would seem to follow that the consequence of obedience must have been everlasting life. In its very nature, death can only be lasting, for its heart and essence consist in separation from God. There can be no such thing as temporary death from which a man may return to life, for when a man is separated from God he is in the bonds of everlasting death. From such a condition he must be rescued, if there is to be a rescue, by God alone. Nor does the rescue from death itself bring life. New life must be given to the one who once was dead, and this new life cannot be generated by man, but in the nature of the case can only be a gift from God. Inasmuch, then, as death is everlasting and inasmuch as the penalty of disobeying God's command with respect to the forbidden tree was everlasting death, it must follow that had man not disobeyed the command of God he would not die. What kind of life, however, would he then possess?

Had man obeyed God he would, as it were, have passed a test. He would have shown that, even though he might not have understood the reason for God's prohibition, nevertheless, inasmuch as God had given the prohibition, he had chosen to obey it. Such a resolve would have been made out of love to God and out of a desire to do his will. Does it not then follow that if disobedience had brought death, obedience would have brought life; and since disobedience brought everlasting death, obedience would have brought everlasting life?[1]

1. Hodge (*ibid.*, p. 123) gives three reasons why the life promised was not mere continuance of existence: '(a) From the fact that the death

The Confession speaks of perfect and personal obedience. And was this not what God required? That the obedience was to be personal cannot be disputed. The prohibition had been made to Adam himself, and he was the one responsible for his actions with respect to eating the fruit of the tree of the knowledge of good and evil. In the very language of the prohibition the second person singular pronoun is employed.

Must the obedience itself, however, be perfect? To ask this question is in reality to answer it. Can we think of the holy God resting satisfied with anything less than perfect obedience? Imperfect obedience is sinful, and sinful acts, even when done in the Name of the Lord, are not pleasing to him. Furthermore, the nature of the prohibition should be noted. Actually the tree of the knowledge of good and evil was in itself a thing indifferent. It was neither good nor evil, but simply one of the trees that God had planted in the garden. Nor would the fruit of this tree in itself in any way bring harm to the eater. From this it would appear that the prohibition demanded upon Adam's part an unreasoned obedience. As Hodge puts it, the command was '. . . plainly designed to be a naked test of obedience, absolute and without limit.' With respect to such a test one cannot think of imperfect or sinful obe-

threatened was not the mere extinction of existence. Adam experienced that death the very day he ate the forbidden fruit. The death threatened was exclusion from the communion of God. The life promised, therefore, must consist in the divine fellowship and the excellence and happiness thence resulting. (b) From the fact that mere existence was not in jeopardy. It is the character, not the fact, of continued existence which God suspended upon obedience. (c) Because the terms 'life' and 'death' are used in the Scriptures constantly to define two opposite spiritual conditions, which depend upon the relation of the soul to God.'

dience. Were one to obey such a test his obedience must be perfect, else his action would be a mockery. Surely the Confession is on good scriptural ground when it speaks of 'perfect and personal obedience.' We may note also that the Confession designates this covenant with Adam and his posterity as the first covenant and characterizes it as a covenant of works. By the term 'first,' reference is not made to order in the eternal councils, but rather to the first covenant that concerned mankind.

By way of conclusion, then it would appear that the Westminster Confession has accurately stated what is taught in the second chapter of Genesis. There is not much point in quarrelling as to whether this divine administration is to be labelled a covenant or not. For our part, we are inclined to believe that the language of the Confession at this point has not gone beyond the Scriptures. Here is an administration that in its origin, establishment, arrangement, and disposition is of God. Furthermore, it is an arrangement that concerns a man and his posterity. Surely it does bear the characteristics of a divine covenant, and we, for our part, have no hesitation in designating it a covenant. On this particular point, we believe that the Confession speaks in accordance with the Scriptures. For our part, we prefer to call this covenant a covenant of life, as does the shorter Catechism, for that word indicates the grand design of the covenant.